heightened consciousness,

cultural revolution,

and curriculum theory

THE PROCEEDINGS OF
THE ROCHESTER CONFERENCE

WILLIAM PINAR
EDITOR

McCutchan Publishing Corporation
2526 Grove Street
Berkeley, California 94704

ISBN: 0-8211-1511-1
Library of Congress Catalog Card Number: 73-17615

PREFACE

It is difficult enough to understand the nature of one's own life in this last third of the twentieth century without attempting to explicate the meaning of our collective life. Yet, being who we are, many of us make the attempt just the same. After all, it is probably a warranted assumption that each dimension or level contributes to the other, so to have some idea where we North Americans are in a social historical sense is probably to be able to make more sense of where I am or you are individually in a biographic sense. Self-understanding—its importance has been underscored since the Ancients. Today it would seem to take on additional significance. But I am ahead of myself.

A number of observers have contended that North American social history discloses a split, discloses that a numerically smaller and chronologically younger group has formed and continues to form which is counter to the dominant culture, to that social collectivity typically the object of study for social historians and for other observers. Further, as you most likely are aware, this group tended to and tends to distinguish itself from the larger group by its customs, its ways of expressing individuality and sociality. Hair length, clothing, diet, vocational and avocational interests, political preferences all tended, at first, simply to differ from current dominant customs, and then to take on a self-affirmative aspect which makes them more than protests. They tend to characterize a culture of North Americans who view the nature of their lives and of their social world differently than do their parents.

This development has, of course, been the subject of both derision and praise. Those predisposed to the latter tended to characterize the development as "the movement," "the greening of America," "the making of a counterculture," and the "cultural revolution." What we are observing, some argued (like Reich and Roszak), is a sudden and radical change in the customs of life that comprise culture. At its most fundamental, the argument continued, it is a change of observable life effected by a change of unobservable life, of inner life, of consciousness. Actions, beliefs, in fact, whole world views which have been held from a particular perspective or similar perspectives are now being viewed from quite different vantage points. So we are witnessing not so much widespread and fundamental changes in external structures (political and institutional ones, for example) but rather profound changes in how these particular external structures are viewed, for example, in consciousness. It is true that these changes in awareness have external manifestations, yet what distinguishes this development is its origin. It comes from within, so to speak, from one's consciousness of self and other, and then moves outward, so to speak, manifesting itself in customs of life-styles, work, and other ways.

Of course, part of the hypothesized reason for this "heightened consciousness" (as it was characterized by those who viewed it favorably) was the presumed sterility of life focused on externals, on the unquestioning acquisition of commonly held values, including that of acquisition itself. To be is to have, to be successful is to have much, but, in any case, one is supposedly consumed by one's consumption.

Of course this *mode d'être* has its manifestations in social science and in the field of education. Somewhat oversimply, it has meant that we focus our investigations on the observable, on what we can readily see, and we identify certain variables and then test to determine their relation to each other and to other variables. Confronted with the complicated phenomena associated with curriculum, its formulation, its development, its implementation, its evaluation, and its justification, we have tended to dwell on external variables and attempted to copy the empirical work of social scientists. Even work that has tended to be conceptual, for example, King and Brownell's well-known effort, still understandably represents cognitive modes and values found in the prevalent culture. Those at work in the field of education and in the subfield of curriculum have of course been prodded for their militant middle-classness (in classic Marxist logic our class membership is presumably the major determinant of our theoretical formulations and of our empirical findings), but the essential nature of our work has changed little.

The work may have remained largely the same, but our attitude toward it has not. Our confidence erodes. Sensitive as many of us are to the tacit and often not so tacit criticism which the development of a counterculture implies (we are their "Parents" in a sense; to us they remain accountable until their twenties, unless, of course, they leave "home"), we talk at rather remarkable lengths about the "importance of what the young are trying to tell us." Yet, given the nature of many of our childhoods, many of us tend to hear mostly the criticism, and our shaky confidence becomes shakier, leaving us rather hopeless, or rather restless, jumping the next proverbial bandwagon, be it values clarification or behavioral objectives, searching (outside ourselves the cultural revolutionary might note) for some certainty, for some sense of legitimate professional and theoretical direction.

So it is no accident, I think, that the question, "What is curriculum theory?" is asked more regularly, if not more ironically. Such questioning belies more than the adolescence of a field and that stage's "search for identity." In one sense, it is cultural dilemma writ small, the manifestation in professional education of the macrocosmic uncertainty. The insistence with which the question is asked indicates the need for more than an answer; it calls for some form of affirmation, so that a question is less crucial, if not inane.

I offer a vignette which further fills in this sketch. New Orleans, 1973. AERA. The Special Interest Group for the Generation and Utilization of Knowledge in Curriculum, cochaired by Edmund Short (Pennsylvania State University) and Paul Klohr (Ohio State University) met to discuss the nature of work done in the field. Mauritz Johnson (State University of New York, Albany) presided at the meeting, which, after a report by Short, became a discussion of the nature of the field. George Beauchamp (Northwestern University), among others, argued for making our work more scientific, for delimiting the areas of inquiry, for reaching consensus on the conceptual, and then for working empirically. James Macdonald (University of North Carolina, Greensboro) and Michael Apple (University of Wisconsin, Madison) argued for the legitimacy of several approaches to the generation and utilization of knowledge in curriculum, particularly for work that could be said to be theoretical although not necessarily in a strict scientific sense of that term. The meeting, while without consensus, was not without frustration. Obviously, the disagreement goes deeper than the manifest content would indicate.

On the surface, of course, the field has been at this point before. One recalls the effort of the Association for Supervision and Curriculum Development in the mid-1960's. That organization established two commissions, one on instructional theory and one on curriculum theory. Each commission was assigned the task of making order out of the two domains, and of suggesting desirable directions for further study. The commission concerned with theory building in instruction moved ahead and in 1968, under the editorship of Ira Gordon, published a set of criteria. These criteria clearly reflected an empirical, scientific mode of inquiry. In effect, the field of instruction was defined by this one approach to theory development.

In contrast, the commission on curriculum theory proved unwilling to delimit the field of curriculum in one way. As a consequence, the commission failed to produce a set of criteria that might have been used to order all curriculum phenomena. At one of the seminars sponsored by the commission in 1965, in Chicago, Elizabeth Maccia, taking a metatheoretical stance, identified four distinct modes of theorizing which she contended were appropriate for theorizing in curriculum. She termed these event theory, formal theory, valuational theory, and praxiological theory.

Other precedents acknowledge several modes of curriculum theory work. Macdonald, in a 1971 piece in the *Journal of Educational Research,* outlined the work being done in the field according to the function theory had. For instance, one group works with theory as a guide to curriculum development. A second group conceives of theory as a scientific endeavor. A third group views the task of theorizing as a matter of reconceptualizing the field.

For example, the 1947 University of Chicago Conference on Curriculum Theory, considered by many as a historical benchmark in the field, can be viewed, using the Macdonald lens, as a discussion of theory as a guide to curriculum development, although it harbingers later work in all three realms. Herrick and Tyler, for instance, in the overview section in *Toward Improved Curriculum Theory,* the publication of the Chicago conference, argue that the task of defensible curriculum theory is threefold: First such theory must identify the critical issues or points in the curriculum development process and their underlying generalizations. Second, curriculum theory must identify the relation between these critical points and their supporting structures. Third, it needs to suggest and forecast the future of approaches made to resolve these issues.

Some of the conceptual work that Herrick and Tyler seemed to be calling for surfaced in the 1967 Ohio State University Conference, in the paper presented by Duncan and Frymier. The empirical interest, as well as the focus on curriculum development, surfaces in the papers presented at the 1969 Stanford University Conference. In the editor's preface to *Confronting Curriculum Reform,* the publication of the Cubberly Conference, Eisner, who chaired the meeting, writes of the need for an empirical science of curriculum development.

In the paper given by B. Othanel Smith at the 1947 Chicago Conference, one finds a kind of foreshadowing of work that appears at the 1967 Ohio State meeting and at the 1973 Rochester meeting. Smith sketches what he sees as four aspects of the educational task in the present era. First is the need for a "new frame of acceptance," a value orientation that is adequate for the age. Second is the need for collective social goals which grant meaning to individual effort and achievement. Third is the necessity of a conceptualization of human nature based upon psychological and sociological theory, which embraces what he calls "new insights into personal and social actions and accomplishments." Fourth, Smith concludes, is the need for new patterns of thinking about social policies and actions, to replace what he saw as the prevalent and obsolete habit of thinking in a linear and compartmentalized fashion, where the attempt is made, for instance, to keep the disciplines in separate spheres.

But what about today? What would come from a conference entitled "Heightened Consciousness, Cultural Revolution, and Curriculum Theory," connecting with conjunctives terms on disparate conceptual levels, levels of both latent and manifest meaning? So I issued invitations to Donald Bateman, Maxine Greene, Dwayne Huebner, James Macdonald, William Pilder, and Robert Starratt.

The conference met May 3-5, 1973, in Rochester. Some one hundred professors and students from several sections of the country attended.

What is there to say of it? Its connections to earlier meetings comes to mind. Macdonald's paper, for instance, almost seems to answer Smith's 1947 call for an adequate normative position.

Bateman's paper concerns itself with collective social and political goals and their discrepancy with actual curriculum materials, as well as with the basic need to become much more politically aware. Greene and Macdonald, as well as Pilder and Pinar, work from a curricular perspective to conceptualize human nature in the light of recent intellectual as well as cultural developments.

Further correspondences appear. The underlying "value gestalt" that characterizes the Chicago collection is essentially a "social needs" orientation. Clearly, it is a point of view within the Dewey tradition of experimentalism and scientific problem solving. Even Smith, who more than the others calls for another sort of value frame, concludes his paper with talk about "human management of a vast social machine." He sees the task of education, in part, as creating a "new personality" type capable of participating in a society which is thus deliberately managed. He also speaks of the knowledge and technique of "social engineering."

In one sense, this is the kind of theoretical talk which Newman and Oliver would ascribe to their view of the "Great Society" approach to problems of curriculum. Charles Hampden-Turner would characterize the language forms as coming from a "borrowed toolbox," with a basically conservative view of the relationship between society and man. Although several of the Rochester papers touched on some of the problems with which Smith dealt, the "value gestalts" which characterized this most recent conference collection differ markedly from Smith's version of experimentalism. The philosophical underlinings of several Rochester papers seem clearly within the realm of Existentialism. In them, man is conceived as the radiating source of meaning. This focus, perhaps most visible in papers by Pilder, Bateman, Greene, and Pinar, can be seen as related to the more general inner focus of the cultural revolution. As you recall, this movement has been viewed as a revolution of consciousness, as radical and profound changes inside people, changing how and what they think and feel, in fact how they view the nature of their lives. It lacks the inherent pessimism of, say, Sartrean Existentialism, but the focuses on inner states as well as on action following from the state, are similar.

As I planned the Rochester meeting, I had not requested that the speakers speak explicitly to the conference theme. That was a task I would take on myself. Yet I expected that I had chosen among the most sensitive in the field, in whose work, however idiosyncratically and seemingly removed, would appear some of the content of the cultural revolution. Further, I hoped that the theme would serve as a possible point of synthesis for the continuing work of those invited. I was not disappointed.

Huebner and Greene have worked persistently on questions of meaning and language, and both extended their position in ways that raised interesting questions for practitioners and theorizers alike. My work, which has been exploring a phenomenological approach that draws heavily on psychoanalytic theory, offered a partial explanation of the conference theme. Bateman and Pilder offered political and cultural analyses. Bateman drew on the work of Freire to support his belief in the need to "demythologize" curriculum. By implication, Pilder makes a compelling case for the creation of intentional communities which might foster what he terms "mutual indwelling." These two theorists urge a fundamental reexamination of the relationship between curriculum, the school, and society. All papers attempt, in some fashion, to deal with internal experience.

I found the conference to have a certain coherence; a sequence developed as I listened, which is preserved in the present order, except for the inclusion of my paper at the beginning, to serve as an introduction to the conference theme. The papers, in a word, moved me, and it was this emotional response which heightened the intellectual one. For me there was a kind of congruence between content and process.

The "lived experience" of the meeting was also with the participants, and some account of their experience is appropriate. Some leaders of the small groups have attempted to describe their work with participants; others have endeavored to respond more explicitly to the papers. Their efforts follow the papers.

It is now four months since the conference, and the emotional sense I took from the meeting has slowly settled, and certain more cognitive impressions remain. The focus of certain curriculum theorizers continue to lie inward. Inner states seem more important than observable behaviors, or at least as important. While the educational process may have much to do with the acquisition of information and the development of usable (and sellable) skills, it also has to do with the cultivation of self-knowledge, of wisdom. That these matters are extraordinarily complicated may mean those who work with them may "lose," temporarily, to the behaviorists, to the social engineers (who may be able to sell the public nearly anything as long as they can demonstrate "a change in behavior"), but only for a while. If the race is to survive these strange times, then it must evolve morally and intellectually; it must evolve in consciousness. The dynamics of much evolution are obscure, yet one has a certain faith that if they can be translated into educational sense, then minds like Huebner's, Greene's, and Macdonald's can so translate.

I had the sense of a group of almost lonely scholars whose coming together was a time of sad celebration of mutual effort, of mutual acknowledgement that, while individual paths may differ markedly, ultimately we seek the same, and that same has something to do with what the phrase "the quality of existence" hints at, something to do with the cultivation of wisdom. This, finally, it seems to me, recalls the theme of consciousness and cultural revolution.

Yet the audience, and a part of me also, had more immediate concerns, and these were left unsatisfied, partly because none of the papers dealt explicitly enough with practitioner-type questions and partly because we may not know how to answer them at this historical point.

Four issues (there were others) kept making themselves heard, and I comment impressionistiscally and briefly.

a. Confidence in schools as liberating institutions. Pilder is unequivocal that schools are hopeless; they can only enslave faculty and students. Bateman seemed similarly unhopeful; schools are extensions of the oppressive, totalitarian capitalist superstructure, and as such can only be expected to continue sexism, classism, and racism. Huebner seems similarly pessimistic, but only in a sense, for he does continue to work with the language of schoolpeople, with the tacit assumption that some sort of amelioration may someday be possible. Greene strikes me as mildly more hopeful; if (and admittedly a crucial if) the teacher is special and he or she is sensitive and intelligent and skillful in the way Greene outlines in her paper, then liberation is more possible. Macdonald is able to assume "centering" might be possible in the context of school. Even so, the hopefulness is decidedly guarded; I found little compelling evidence, in Macdonald's paper or in anyone else's to alter my pessimistic view on this matter.

b. Shape of future reform. Only the barest outlines of that shape were drawn. In part it must be theoretical, involving a reworking of the language we employ to describe phenomena associated with curriculum. It must be political, involving not only structural changes in the teacher-student and the school-society relationships, but involving also a politically sensitive analysis of curriculum materials. It must as well be psychological, involving a shift in focus on one's "center," one's inner states.

c. Commitment to public education. Pilder's paper clearly undercut the traditional commitment to public educational institutions. Although other papers were not explicit, one sensed a frustration, at times almost a hopelessness, at the possibility of significant reformation. Pilder told us that schools were no longer a milieu that could foster the development of self, of awareness, of will. We have reached a point where we must leave public institutions to personally manifest cultural transformations. One left the conference uncertain about the possibilities of public education.

d. Future of "scientism" in the field of education. It is not that the speakers dismissed scientism; they ignored it. None of them appeared especially interested in working in so-called scientific ways; their mode of inquiry was philosophical and logical. I would guess this is no accident. The speakers were attempting to deal with inner phenomena: consciousness, transcendence, liberation, centering. "Scientism" may continue to prove more helpful to educators interested in the measurements of observable, behavioral changes, but it has and will probably continue to prove less helpful to those attempting to chronicle internal changes.

I place my paper first, in the hope that its placement there will more fully introduce these notions of heightened consciousness and cultural revolution than I have been able to do here. Then following is Starratt's sense of the state of the field, and then, in the order they were given, the papers of Huebner, Bateman, Greene, Macdonald, and Pilder. The reactions—papers of the small-group leaders—conclude the collection.

I wish to acknowledge the support and assistance of my colleagues at the University of Rochester, especially Professor James I. Doi, Dean of the College of Education, Professor Ellsworth S. Woestehoff, Chairman of the Department of Curriculum, Teaching and Supervision, Professor Eleanore Larson, Professor Thomas Hill, and Professor William Lowe, who also helped editorially. Of course I am grateful as well to the speakers, to the leaders of small groups, to the other participants, and to Donald Parry and his staff at the University Conference Office. I wish to give special thanks to David Purpel, Professor of Education at the University of North Carolina at Greensboro, who assisted me editorially, and to Paul Klohr, Professor of Education at the Ohio State University, whose original suggestion and assistance with planning and invitations helped make the meeting possible.

CONTRIBUTORS

Donald R. Bateman is Associate Professor of Humanities Education at the Ohio State University.

Maxine Greene is Professor of English and Educational Philosophy at Teachers College, Columbia University, and the author, most recently, of *Teacher as Stranger*.

Dwayne Huebner is Professor of Curriculum and Teaching at Teachers College, Columbia University, and the author of several essays.

James Macdonald is Professor of Education at the University of North Carolina at Greensboro, and the author of numerous articles.

William Pilder was Assistant Professor of Education at Indiana University. Now Mr. Pilder works in a Montessori school and lives with friends in Greenwich, Connecticut.

William Pinar is Assistant Professor of Education at the University of Rochester, and the editor of *Shadowgraphs: Sketches from a Suburb*.

Robert Starratt is Associate Principal of Regis High School and Professor of Education at Regis College in Denver, Colorado. He is the coauthor, with Thomas Sergiovanni, of *Emerging Patterns of Supervision: Human Perspectives*.

Charles Beegle is Associate Professor of Education at the University of Virginia.

Paul R. Klohr is Professor of Curriculum and Foundations at the Ohio State University, and the author of numerous articles.

Eleanore Larson is Professor of Education at the University of Rochester.

William T. Lowe is Professor of Education at the University of Rochester, and the author of several articles and books.

Robert Osborn is Associate Professor of Education at the University of Rochester. Professor Osborn has lectured on educational philosophy in both England and Japan; currently he is coauthoring a book on issues in education, which will appear in 1974.

Francine Shuchat Shaw studied English education and film at the Ohio State University. Currently she is Assistant Professor in the Department of Film at the Rochester Institute of Technology.

George Willis is Assistant Professor of Education at the University of Rhode Island. His major interests are in curriculum theory and the development of thought about the curriculum field. He has contributed to *Curriculum Theory Network*.

CONTENTS

I. HEIGHTENED CONSCIOUSNESS, CULTURAL REVOLUTION,
AND CURRICULUM THEORY: AN INTRODUCTION
William F. Pinar   1

II. CURRICULUM THEORY: CONTROVERSY, CHALLENGE,
AND FUTURE CONCERNS   *Robert J. Starratt, S.J.*   16

III. TOWARD A REMAKING OF CURRICULAR LANGUAGE
Dwayne Huebner   36

IV. THE POLITICS OF CURRICULUM   *Donald R. Bateman*   54

V. COGNITION, CONSCIOUSNESS, AND CURRICULUM
Maxine Greene   69

VI. A TRANSCENDENTAL DEVELOPMENTAL IDEOLOGY OF
EDUCATION   *James B. Macdonald*   85

VII. IN THE STILLNESS IS THE DANCING   *William F. Pilder*   117

REACTIONS

A. An All-American Small Group in Search of an Electric
Kool-Aid Acid Theory of Curriculum   *Robert L. Osborn*   131

B. Reactions of a Group Leader   *Charles Beegle*   138

C. Some Reactions   *William T. Lowe*   142

D. Reactions to the Conference   *George Willis*   151

E. The Listeners   *Francine Shuchat Shaw*   156

F. Report on Discussions of Group F   *Eleanore E. Larson*   161

G. Reflections on the Conference   *Paul R. Klohr*   166

I. HEIGHTENED CONSCIOUSNESS, CULTURAL REVOLUTION, AND CURRICULUM THEORY: AN INTRODUCTION

William F. Pinar

Permit me to attempt to dispel my discomfort by disclosing it, my discomfort at working at such a broad conceptual level, as the title suggests. My state derives from these considerations. First, my sense is that these matters which I propose to discuss are less familiar to many of us than topics more typically associated with studies in theoretical formulations of curriculum. Related to this sense of our collective awareness and understanding of these matters is the decidedly inchoate stage of my work in these areas. These concepts, like many others similarly abstract and global, are complicated, and at times one feels one's tools may not prove adequate. Yet one makes the attempt, moved by a sensed significance of these matters for many interested in curriculum. One's diffidence in this regard is further heightened by the speculative nature of these observations and proposals which are to follow, and by their tangential relation to the disciplines from which I began my study, that is to say, education, specifically curriculum theory, and English, especially twentieth-century British literature, and, more recently, studies in psychoanalysis, particularly the work of Carl Jung and R. D. Laing (it may not prove unfair to Dr. Jung to connect his name with Dr. Laing's with a conjunctive) and in some areas of psychology. Thus where I began, but now, realizing that my attempts to understand the phenomena that tend to be identified as countercultural or culturally revolutionary, phenomena which, as one would suspect, manifest themselves sociologically and psychologically, as well as historically and educationally, and realizing that my formulations were not essentially literary, nor curricular, nor, more broadly, educational (although they are, obviously, precedents to this sort of inquiry in the field), nor psychological, nor historical, I attempted to understand and justify the effort thusly. While some notions psychoanalytic in origin hold considerable exploratory power, none I would recall

provided me with sufficient range and depth to conceptually frame
the phenomena which interested me. So I found myself forced to
employ notions essentially outside any discipline.

Further, I thought, if indeed this development known as cultural
revolution does harbinger, as some observers have contended, a new
era, a different ontological and epistemological order than Western
man has known for several centuries, then most assuredly one might
justifiedly find oneself outside one's discipline, seeking a notion of
sufficient magnitude to order such considerations. Of course, it is we
who must decide if such a strategy has been warranted.

Many of us find ourselves attempting to understand the complicated phenomena we observe in classrooms. To this end we have
studied the nature of knowledge, particularly codified knowledge
and its embodiment in artifacts, the nature of human beings, of the
actors involved and the complex interactions or operations of actors
among actors, and with artifacts. The obvious and immediate context
within which these phenomena occur is the classroom, and while the
determinants we identify in classrooms (such as pedagogical technique) are powerful in their effects, there would appear to be less
obvious, less immediate, yet possibly equally powerful factors operative. We can designate such factors historical or cultural in nature. To
restrict one's view to the obvious and to the immediate is, it seems to
me, to risk nearsightedness. One can see close at hand, but forces in
the distance, whose influence on the close at hand may be compelling, are blurred if recognizable at all.

Of course, to restrict one's view to the distant is to risk farsighted-
ness, that is, obscuring the consequences of forces that are peculiar
to the situation under study. To view through lenses that permit
both perspectives simultaneously (which, by the way, would, it
seems to me, be an instance of heightened consciousness) might permit an adequate understanding of the dynamics of these elements of
curriculum: actors, artifacts, operations.

So, with the danger at least acknowledged if not exorcised, let me
get on with my observations of developments in the distance.

SEVERANCE FROM SELF

While alienation has been a theme in imaginative literature and in
philosophy for centuries, its expression in the twentieth century by

some Western artists and philosophers seems particularly insistent. Heidegger's sense of "shipwrecked," and Eliot's sense of "hollow men" dwelling in a "wasteland" convey this sense of malaise. Now many of us experience what might have seemed, in years past, this expression of a particular literary or intellectual subculture. Terms like estrangement, dehumanization, and madness have at times been employed to characterize our condition. At an earlier time I tried to understand, from a psychoanalytic perspective identified with R. D. Laing, how a certain form of schooling was both a consequence and determinant of this dehumanization. My sense of the term is this: for reasons still dimly understood, man, particularly so-called modern man, is estranged and severed from his Self. Self is understood in the Jungian sense, as more than the ego or conscious "I" of the personality; it is, I think, roughly equivalent to what Don Juan (in the Castaneda books) refers to as essence. Thus, man, the conscious "I" we identify as ego, is somehow severed from his self, which is hidden from his ego; it is, in part, his unconscious. That is to say, then, that man is partially unaware of himself; he is not himself; he is dehumanized. What to talk like this means I hope to at least partially disclose.

This severance from self appears to have the effect of forcing us to search for dignity and satisfaction outside ourselves. Ignoring the inner regions, intrigued by the elaborate labyrinthine exterior world, many of us spend our lives searching for meaning outside ourselves. While such symbolic attempts at satisfaction, at "actualization," at times achieve their aims, the achievement is usually short lived, as transient as feeling, or as thought, as transitory as prominence, whether in the lives of one's countrymen, or in the lives of one's children.

This symbolic search, which amounts to what Sartre terms one's project, forces what has been called a literary awareness and organization of one's life. This literary or what we might call "movie" awareness is a peculiar manifestation of our condition, which, if described adroitly, I think, may permit us to get closer to the heart of this matter of dehumanization, and, conversely in a sense, of "heightened consciousness." From this literary or "movie" perspective one is a character, presumably the main one, or the "star," in a novel or movie of one's own making (or so it might seem). As it is in the movies, the significance of one's life is a function of certain episodes or adventures. Most films and novels, of course, consist of a series of "telling" episodes or adventures. Slow and sometimes boring Sunday afternoons, for example, are infrequently portrayed. Although that be the case, interestingly one critic's praise of the recent film "Sunday, Bloody Sunday" had to do with its portrayal of the "in-between" of life, not the periods of despair or of excitement, but of the middle range where most of us live most of the time. Those periods, for many of us, are obscure; their meaning, if any, lies in their relation to memorable episodes past or future. For Sartre, for example, the moment takes on importance in the context of one's project. For Heidegger, it is poignant awareness of death that gives this moment urgency and significance. In neither case does the moment have portent in and of itself. Its importance derives from its relation to other, more memorable moments.

One notes this "literary organization" or, if you will, "movie consciousness" when listening to people describe their lives. One tells stories, and tells them as if they were ultimate reality. In Sartre's novel *Nausea*, in a passage that might give access to this point, Antoine Roquentin, the narrator, explains:

"This is what I thought: for the most banal even to become an adventure, you must (and this is enough) begin to recount it. This is what fools people: a man is always a teller of tales; he lives surrounded by his stories and the stories of others, he sees everything that happens to him through them; and he tries to live his own life as if he were telling a story.

But you have to choose: live or tell . . .

Nothing happens while you live. The scenery changes, people come in and go out, that's all. There are no beginnings. Days are tacked on days without rhyme or reason, an interminable, monotonous addition. From time to time you make a semitotal: you say: I've been travelling for three years, I've been in Bouville for three years. Neither is there any end: you never leave a woman, a friend, a city in one go. And then everything looks alike: Shanghai, Moscow, Algiers, everything is the same after two weeks. There are moments—rarely—when you make a landmark, you realize you're going with a woman, in some messy business. The time of a flash. After that, the procession starts again, you begin to add up hours and days: Monday, Tuesday, Wednesday, April, May, June. 1924, 1925, 1926.

That's living. But everything changes when you tell about life; it's a change no one notices: the proof is that people talk about true stories. As if there could possibly be true stories . . ."[1]

This perspective is a revealing manifestation of our absorption at the levels of personality, at the tip of the iceberg. It indicates our absorption with the observable, with the external, and our comparative ignorance of what lies beneath the surface, with our inner lives, with our essence. The possibility, briefly outlined, is that with the development of the transcendental ego or the "third eye," one is able to observe, to some extent, one's ego, the "I" of the personality, involved in the affairs of the world, with plans for, say, career, family, and so on, the components of life in the present historical period. With knowledge of self, however, with disclosure of the unconscious, one develops this transcendent perspective, this "heightened consciousness," and one is able, in some instances, to choose or write one's own script, or come to understand how the complex interplay of forces—psychological, sociological, and historical—in nature converge to write the script you act out, to form the particular personality you have, with the particular work you are to perform in the world. It is a sign of our uprootedness from our selves that we tell stories as if they were true, as if they portrayed an ultimate reality. Without the anchoring of being in and from oneself, one is indeed shipwrecked, or, to change images, hollow, a character on a stage.

Thus pulled by the depths, yet aware of only the waves, we bulwark ourselves horizontally, as it were, by the colluding confirmation of others. Uprooted from our essence, we require securing of another sort, a stability derived from the steadying gaze of others. This symbolic attempt at groundedness takes other forms than interpersonal ones, such as ideological adherence, but it is this particular form that seems problematic to many in this day.

Many of us find the support of others necessary to self-esteem and security. While the need for acceptance of others may be limited to significant others (like family, friends, work associates), the need for such confirmation is understood to be revealingly if not oppressively intense. Kierkegaard notes in his *Diary* what he terms the "herd instinct" and the problematic nature of solitude. Yet in solitude, Kierkegaard continues, lies the true measure of an individual. However, alone, one is likely to feel uneasy, restless, compelled to "do something" to "pass the time."

In solitude ones' Self, buried from view by programming or conditioning, and maintained from view, in part, by the collusion of others, threatens to intrude, to raise questions, so to speak, concerning the plot of the movie, the performance of the actor, and the congruence of both with the Self.

One notes a certain hurriedness to smiles and confirming remarks among interlocutors. Disagreements take on an exaggerated importance, tending to act as disconformation of one's sense of self. When one's sense of self is importantly contingent upon others' acceptance, as it must be when it is severed from itself, and/or when one's script calls for characteristic and anticipated responses from others, one is often understandably uneasy, and disappointed. An awareness of these matters, particularly of scripts, appears to comprise, in part, heightened consciousness.

CULTURAL REVOLUTION AND HEIGHTENED CONSCIOUSNESS

For reasons of which we are dimly aware, there appears to be a distinguishable hiatus in the evolution of Western man, particularly on the North American continent. This gap has, of course, been the subject of considerable attention from commentators of various sorts. Charles Reich and George Leonard, for example, offer essentially journalistic observations and impressions, while academicians like Louis Feuer, Theodore Roszak, and, more perceptively, I think, Herbert Marcuse, offer somewhat more substantive analysis. At whatever conceptual level and to whatever degree of intellectual sophistication, accounts are being written that describe or propose the development of an alternative culture on the North American continent, and, to a lesser extent, in Western Europe, sufficiently distinguishable from the dominant culture to warrant descriptors like "generation gap" and "cultural revolution."

There are several difficulties involved in understanding the nature of cultural revolution in this country. One involves a certain anger and resentment that would appear to prompt some writing countercultural in origin. The motive in these cases seems to be to punish as much as it is to inform. Another difficulty derives from mistaking certain signs of countercultural membership, for example, hair length, as a substantive element. This mistaking appearance for reality, coupled with what appears to be naïveté, has resulted in prognostications regarding a "greening" and other presumably welcome transformations of North American society, despite compelling evidence to the contrary. Such accounts, needless to say, quickly disappoint and disinterest.

A more serious difficulty has to do with the inaccessibility of the most evolved forms of the cultural revolutionary to those of us in institutional life. As a faculty member, for example, one has access to certain kinds of information. One's sources have to do with written material of several types, with one's colleagues, and with one's students. One notes certain easily observable characteristics of one's students, but few of us, I suspect, have sufficient contacts with those young people who no longer seek their fortunes in academia to observe what seems to me to be the heart of the matter. In other words, those of us in institutional life are able to observe institutional manifestations of historical and cultural developments. However, when the kernel of the matter in question surfaces elsewhere, say in rural New England or in the rural Southeast, the academician is at a decided disadvantage. He finds himself relying on written material, which is, as I have noted, problematic in this case.

My fortunes would have it that many of those to whom I am close have, in several senses, left institutional life, and several reside in the geographical areas mentioned. As these people make their occasional visits to me, they bring others. These meetings plus readings in matters countercultural, have resulted in the observations and speculations about which you hear now.

The heart of the matter appears to reside in what we might call perceptual orientation, or in ontological* rootedness. One recalls Reisman's famous distinction between inner- and outer-directedness. This distinction is useful here, if understood somewhat differently. Attention to ideology, to tradition, to social expectation is understood to be attention to matters outside oneself. One is reminded of Kierkegaard's "ethical man," who decides problematic issues by referring to rules. The counterculturist, relying on information provided at once by instinct, emotion, intelligence, attempts to refer to himself. On the whole, he tends not to rely on social rules, acquired moral systems, which is to say, he tends not to rely on the computating and logical capabilities of the mind, rather on the symbolizing and synthesizing capabilities. Meaning, potency, indeed, behavior tend to derive from within; and, in this regard, one psychoanalyst, who appears to have some intellectual currency among some counterculturists, has written that "any meaning derived from a source

---

*While Sartre, Heidegger, Tillich, and others employ ontology in its philosophic sense, I use it as the best adverbial or adjectival form of "being."

outside our acts murders us."[2] The source of behavior would appear, then, to be the distinguishing factor. The dominant culture is understood to be preoccupied with the observable.

Some observers, not entirely for intellectual convenience, locate the origins of "the movement" in the late 1950's and early 1960's in the San Francisco Bay area. There, young people, soon to be designated hippies, frequently through the use of lysergic acid diethylamide (LSD), apparently increased their awareness of their interior lives, of what Heidegger has termed the *Lebensewelt*. One major effect of ingesting this substance evidently was (is) to force to the surface psychic material that had (has) heretofore been obscured. In other words, one is forced to examine certain of the contents of one's unconscious. Concomitantly, as the strength of one's mechanisms of defense is diminished, one tends to become more open, and hence more vulnerable, to the various elements that comprise the ambience, both internal and external. Of course, if any of these elements are experienced as threatening to one's ego or to the "I" of the personality, then the probability of what is called a "bad trip" is increased. One legitimately generalizable effect of LSD would appear to be a heightened awareness of one's interior regions.

Much has been made of the seemingly casual lifestyles of hippies, their sexual behavior, and so on. These matters can be understood as a particular historical and sociological consequence of the loosening of individuals' attachment to currently popularized and conditioned ontological modes. Of course, with some whose motives originate outside themselves, these behaviors may be understood as sexually permissive and socially irresponsible.

Attractive to possibilities observed, and moved as well, one suspects, by a certain rebelliousness, many young people have copied behaviors of these culturally revolutionary. However, in such cases (characterized by imitation), the ontological shift from external to internal has not occurred. Such persons remain outer-directed, and status systems are observed to have been merely changed rather than extinguished. Length of hair, antiwork attitudes, sexual promiscuity, and amount and kinds of drugs ingested become, for such persons, the new signs of status. Clearly such people are incorrectly understood as cultural revolutionary. However, such people are more accessible than the others to the media, hence better known, and they provide evidence that nothing truly substantively countercultural is occurring.

Viewed then, *au fond,* as an ontological shift from external to internal, an attempt to connect the ego with the unconscious and transcending both, one appreciates the importance of the widespread interest in various Eastern philosophic and religious systems presumably designed to aid one to identify oneself. Perhaps most familiar is the interest in what is called Transcendental Meditation, a practice not limited to those outside institutional life. Other meditative practices, less familiar perhaps to many of us, include Zazen, the Zen Buddhist meditation; various forms of meditation associated with Kundalini and Hatha Yogas; and practices associated with the work of the Russian mystic Georges Gurdjieff.

Jacob Needleman has chronicled this increasing interest in what he terms the "new religions." Zen Buddhist centers in Tassajara, California, in New York City, Rochester, and Sharon Springs, New York, and a newly opened center in Minneapolis illustrate a continually strengthened interest in Zen practice. Students of Gurdjieff are found throughout the world, including a communal arrangement south of Rochester, as well as groups in Rochester, Boston, and New York. Transcendental meditators number in the thousands, and regional centers have been established. Instruction in Kundalini's and Hatha Yogas is available in most cities of moderate size.

My impression is that this interest is not faddish. Nor is it an uncharacteristic or exceptional development limited to a few religious zealots. I suspect that it is this interest that is at the heart of the cultural revolution. Understood as the extension of the shift from external to internal, as, in fact, the most advanced evolutionary form of that shift, one comes to understand seemingly unrelated and unintelligible phenomena associated with this notion of cultural revolution.

Consider, for example, its relation to the use of drugs. Many, if not most, young people's rite of passage into the counterculture involves the ingestion of drugs. Almost regardless of the drug used, the stated motive of the user is often to "get high." Some components of this state appear to be: deepened relaxation; diminishing of the power of defense mechanisms; in some cases, a heightened awareness of sensory mechanisms, as well as psychic ones; and increased sensitivity to one's physical interpersonal context. The effects may be interpreted as beneficial; they may not. The telling point is the expressed need to "get high." Andrew Weil argues that such a need is psychobiologic in nature. Whether that be true or not, one's sense is that many counterculturists regard this need as a function of discontentment with a presumably normal state of consciousness. While many employ drugs like LSD and marijuana for recreational motives, others, and I suspect those more internally directed, often use these drugs in an older sense of the word recreational, that is, to re-create one's view of one's self. Led away from oneself, one's perceptual locus is outside oneself. One is stuck, so to speak, in one's mechanisms of defense, identified with one's persona or mask. To aid the shift, to attempt to bring one's attentiveness inside, to loosen the identification with the "I" of personality, many employ these substances. One gets high, more in touch with one's center, one's essence, with who one is, in the Jungian sense. One is able, on occasion, to reach a perceptual point from where one's personality can be an "object" of observation. This nonevaluative observer is what has been called in Western philosophy, particularly in the phenomenological philosophy of Husserl, the transcendental ego. With the emergence of this perspective, one can understand the conditioned and seemingly fortuitous nature of that construct—personality—which one offers to the public world. One has a sense of an "I" that, Heidegger and Sartre to the contrary, is not equivalent to the embodied ego that has projects, has affairs, and so on. That is a world obviously constructed, and hence historically and culturally contingent and transitory. Typically it is a mechanistic world, a world of stimulus-response, the world in which most of us dwell most of the time. Yet "high" one understands the possibility of another, if you will, level of being, a possibility of freedom and volition, that might transcend, in some fashion I dimly understand, the bondage of the public world we know. Yet the route to what must sound like the "promised land" is understood not to lie in political work, economic restructuring, or in education as it is commonly understood today. The route is not understood to lie in the external, public world of social and historical construction. Heretical as it has to sound to many of us, the route is understood to lie within; in part, in making contact with oneself. The way to improve the public world, in short, is to improve oneself. Hardly a new idea, it has its roots in the various great religions of the world, yet its manifestation in the lives of North Americans at mid-twentieth century is indeed interesting and starting, yet intelligible, if understood as an attempt to fill, if you will, a metaphysical vacuum that has persisted since the death of God in the nineteenth century.

As I understand this matter, it is not that, say, political reform is necessarily doomed to fail. It is possible to ameliorate our condition in that fashion, yet the possibility appears to depend on the motive behind such behavior, and the spirit in which it is done. If done to prosecute others, to dethrone or destroy, figuratively or literally, the "opposition," then clearly those involved remain stuck in a world of "our side"-"their side," a we/they polarity that, argues the counter-culturist, cannot result in a general improvement of the human condition. Those in the "winners circle" change, but the fact of winners and losers remains. If, on the other hand, political work is done consciously as a behavioral manifestation of who one is, is done, as it were, for oneself, then the probability of genuinely furthering consequences would seem stronger.

So one comes to understand what first might seem an enigmatic apoliticalness of many countercultural. Of course, many of the young do political work. Many, I understand, have returned to home communities or remained in ones they have adopted, and work in the lower rungs of the political organizational hierarchy, attempting to infiltrate, to transform the political structures from within. Others attempt to establish their own structures, their own bases from which to work. An example of the latter type might be the group which publishes the well-known radical publication *Vocations for Social Change*. In both broad categories of young, the evident assumption is that political work can help to transform the public world.

The less political and more culturally revolutionary might agree, but, as we have noted, insist that such a possibility of transformation is strengthened if the work is conducted self-rememberedly, from one's center, as an expression of oneself.

Focusing one's energies and one's attention exclusively on others is acknowledged as possibly a self-evasive device, permitting one to avoid, say, the "disadvantaged" or "oppressed" elements of one's own life. Especially if the politico has little or no sense of doing the work for himself, but only for others, and at times these "others" have not even requested the particular assistance the politico intends to give, is the suspicion of the cultural revolutionary given rise.

Related to this apparent apoliticalness of many is the notion that gets aphoristically expressed thusly. One cannot fight evil. One can only be good. Evil is fought by being good. Harshness, then, is seen as harshness, hatred as hatred, regardless of the political or

educational objective to which the emotion is presumably subordi-
nated.

Thus the much-heralded movement "back to the country," the
establishment, in evidently increasing numbers, of communal farms,
a development chronicled by such observers as Robert Houriet, Ray
Mungo, Richard Atcheson, and Keith Melville. The notion itself is
not new, of course; one is reminded, for example, of Robert Owen's
work with experimental communities some 130 years earlier. What
differs, one surmises, is the number of people involved, and possibly
the social and economic origins of those involved. One's impression is
that many, possibly most, of these new "farmers" are the children of
America's middle and upper-middle and professional classes. They till
the soil in New England, in the Southeast, in the Northwest, attempting, we are told, to experience an organic relation to the planet they
inhabit.

There are other reasons cited for this migration from suburban and
urban areas to rural ones. A sensed estrangement from one's work is
a factor. Growing one's own food is labor whose motives and consequences take on a clarity and concreteness that many jobs in the
dominant culture do not permit. As well, the interpersonal alienation
understood to be caused in part by the competitive market place
forces many to the country. Usually with little outside income, co-
operativeness becomes a necessity. Then, of course, one, in most
cases, has chosen one's work associates. This attempt at a new style
"extended family" is experienced as more interpersonally gratifying
than the atomized familial arrangements existent in the dominant
culture. Jung wrote, to suggest another reason, that, in times of
estrangement from self, the earth takes on "magical and fascinating
properties." It represents, he writes, the contents of the unconscious.
To till the soil is to work with one's unconscious. And, on an even
broader conceptual level, the rural communal movement may be an
atrophying culture's attempt to cultivate future survivors. The only
partially consciously conceived holocaust, environmental, or political, or economic, or some combination of these origin, is understood
as an externalization, an unconsciously perceived threat of destruction from within.

So a stretch of the cultural revolution begins to fill itself in. Obscure because its clearest manifestations typically occur far from
academia and because those to whom academicians often have access

share the external signs but not the substance of the counterculture, also obscure due to a tendency toward what we might call a scriptless existence and an attitude toward scripts and especially currently common scripts that makes dialogue with those in the dominant culture often poignantly problematic, and while the result of forces immediately social and distantly historical, a movement most deeply understood the race's, at least those elements of the race found on the North American continent, attempt to fill, as it were, a metaphysical vacuum with an inner substance that would seem to be ontological in nature, the movement can legitimately be understood as cultural revolution, consisting of a shift in directedness manifestations of which are unusually considered cultural (in the broad anthropological sense): dress, manner, sexual behavior, living arrangements, careers, and so forth.

At the heart of it is this matter of consciousness. Heightened consciousness, often first experienced with hallucinogenic substances like LSD, sustained and developed by certain meditative practices and by certain lifestyles, meaning, in part, a congruence and integration of conscious and unconscious elements, and at least an exploration of Self, an attempt to render the unconscious conscious, to reclaim the instinctual and sensory bases of human life, presumed to be atrophied in the modern age, it is a transcendence of one-dimensional being, one illustration of which is what we have somewhat jocularly called "movie consciousness." Heightened consciousness thus involves a certain distance from one's script, a lessened identification with the ego that has its being in the public world. That distance involves what Eastern systems have termed the "third eye," and what in Western philosophy has been called the "transcendental ego."

In a certain sense, the counterculture itself can be understood as the unconscious of modern Western civilization. The term underground, which has been used to refer to this development although not exclusively associated with it (one thinks of Dostoevsky's *Underground Man*), does indicate, in a spatial sense, what lies underneath the surface. And some behavior exhibited by counterculturists and some behavior that is not yet projected onto them is an indication of this possible relation to the dominant culture.

Understood in this way, the attitude we in the prevailing culture take, we who are the "ego," and particularly we educators (who, in some ways, it might be said, represent the superego of society) take toward those counter to us and often hidden from us will be interesting and disclosing. Will we recognize the counterculture and cultural revolution for what they are? Will we suppress the information? Will we attempt to integrate the message with our own, and is integration of this sort possible? It will, no doubt, be interesting to observe.

CURRICULUM THEORY

For those of us interested in explicating the nature of the phenomena we observe in classrooms and for those of us who concern ourselves with the nature of curricular intentions, an understanding of a cultural phenomenon such as this will obviously provide an additional dimension to one's study.

For example, in a statistical study, the variables identified may be of a different order, once viewed, say, from a frame of inner/outer. Further, while public school students do tend to be less evolved manifestations of the counterculture, they do tend to fall along some continuum with, say, Zen students at one end, and, say, some military officials at another. If indeed, the young are evolving toward an inner orientation, then one will be able to anticipate or at least understand developments in the future.

Even within the well-worn, and for many, useless, Taylor rationale, countercultural versions of man, society, and knowledge would yield, one would expect, the selection of quite different "learning experiences" than, say, more traditional conceptualizations.

What interests me particularly is this notion of inner/outer. If indeed this idea of inner orientation represents, as it were, a metaphysical and ontological response to the modern age, if indeed this orientation might permit a recognition, an exploration, and possibly a disclosure of the unconscious, both collective and individual, thus the evolution of a more integrated, hence more intelligent, more moral human being, then this matter takes on a significance that is staggering.

My understanding of this matter is obviously incipient and partial. Yet the possibility, which is, of course, the possibility of what we have called humanization, is intriguing enough to warrant the expenditure of considerable intellectual energy. There seem to me to be two "next steps."

1. Continued, more detailed explication of the phenomena of cultural revolution and heightened consciousness. A further examination of the viability of the conceptual frame of inner/outer orientation as an explicative device for understanding the crucial distinction between the dominant culture and the counterculture. Development of linkages with related disciplines, particularly with psychoanalysis and psychology, but possibly as well with literature and philosophy.

2. The design and evaluation of experimental curricula which will attempt to explore the inner life, hence to underscore and possibly aid an ontological shift from outer to inner. The sketch of one such curricular proposal, although still in an inchoate stage, is my notion of a psychosocial-based humanities curriculum, with opportunities for intense interpersonal encounter, for solitude, as well as for study in the traditional areas of humanities literature, music, dance, and so on.

Another possible curricular design model, and one that might be considered for a graduate program in what we might someday call phenomenological curriculum, are extant Ph.D. programs whose orientations are phenomenological, that is, focus on inner experience as well as outer or public experience.

It seems to this student of curriculum that, while the possibilities for rearrangement of curriculum structures and strategies have not been exhausted, they have been exhausting, and one at times hopes for rest before the next packaged proposal makes its appearance. Perhaps it is time, as the counterculturist might suggest, to direct our study inward, and to see what we can see.

NOTES

1. Jean-Paul Sartre, *Nausea*, tr. Lloyd Alexander (New York: New Directions, 1964). Copyright 1964 by New Directions Publishing Corporation. Reprinted by permission.

2. David Cooper, *The Death of the Family* (New York: Pantheon, 1971).

II. CURRICULUM THEORY: CONTROVERSY, CHALLENGE, AND FUTURE CONCERNS

Robert J. Starratt, S.J.

This chapter will be similar to a pause for a deep breath to get our adrenalin moving, a look around the terrain to take our bearings, a checking of a map for familiar landmarks before beginning a journey. In undertaking a discussion of curriculum theory we do not necessarily have to start with the Garden of Eden, but we might be well advised to review the current state of the field, take account of where we are, and underline current promising developments as well as current ambiguous or unproductive points of view.

In reviewing the current state of the field of curriculum theory and practice, we can receive some assistance from already completed studies and commentaries. Professor Louise Tyler has reviewed recent literature dealing with various conceptions and definitions of curriculum, with theory and research in curriculum, and with curriculum planning, topics of curriculum, and evaluation in a rather comprehensive, selected guide to curriculum literature.[1] A recent curriculum report from The National Association of Secondary School Principals describes succinctly various aspects of alternative curricular programs in alternative schools.[2] Professor Joseph Schwab gives his impressions of the state of the field in his essay, *The Practical: A Language for Curriculum.*[3] In a chapter of the book, *Emerging Patterns of Supervision,* I also reviewed the state of the field, commenting especially on the emphases on the disciplines of knowledge as the central focus of curriculum development.[4] An earlier essay by James Macdonald contains some cogent remarks about myths current in curriculum and instruction, and those remarks still seem valid in our current appraisal of the curriculum field.[5]

Rather than repeat what has been said in these works, I review three unresolved controversies about emphases in curriculum theory. Then I challenge Joseph Schwab's proposition about the need to divert our energies away from theoretical concerns toward practical concerns, and, finally, I offer some proposals for change in curriculum theory.

CONTROVERSY

Two competing schools, which I would classify as the "Behaviorists" and the "Humanists," receive much of the attention in current literature related to curricular concerns. Among the behaviorists I would list Skinner, Popham, Flanders, Gagné, and Bloom. Among the humanists I would list Heubner, Macdonald, Foshay, Coombs, Rogers, Greene, and Frazier. While the scholars in both schools express a variety of points of view, what seems to differentiate the two schools is, on the one hand, the behaviorists' attempts to establish empirically verifiable links between teacher-student interaction, prescribed course sequences, and logical and rationally definable states of knowledge or student learning. On the other hand, the humanists' insist that personal, moral, and aesthetic development should occupy at least as much concern as intellectual development. The behaviorists are more concerned with statistically valid research on the improved effectiveness of instruction in reaching predefined cognitive understandings and skill levels. The humanists reply that reality is too multidimensional to be treated in this reductionist fashion and that learning, as it relates to the total developing consciousness of the individual, is also too multidimensional and idiosyncratic to be profitably analyzed by limited statistical correlations that cannot capture the simultaneous and preconscious nature of learning that is continuously taking place. And, even if behaviorists could analyze learning behavior at this complex level through computerized wiring of multiform simultaneous responses that children make to instructional exercises and curricular materials, the humanists would consider this an unnecessary proof of the unique individuality of every student, a proposition they already hold to be self-evident.

Some behaviorists, like Benjamin Bloom,[6] do not appear to be as narrow-minded as many humanists might believe. Rather, they have taken a rather hard-headed approach to learning and seem to be saying: Look, I cannot study everything all at once; instead, I am trying to take a look at the possibility of children mastering some skills and basic understandings. Yes, probably there are any number of other variables involved in learning, and there is more complex learning going on all the time inside of students. But some students do not acquire mastery of even very basic skills that form the building blocks for more complex learning, skills like the use of language syntax and reading. I am trying to discover effective ways to promote mastery at least in these areas. Our research seems to show that, if you alter the time requirements, improve instructional communications, and specify what precisely it is you are trying to get students to do so that they know when they're making progress, we can demonstrate cognitive and emotional growth.

With that kind of interpretation, the humanists have very little quarrel as long as the behaviorists do not universalize or absolutize their research findings as the one or complete explanation of all human learning, or claim that their definitions of specific behavioral outcomes encompass the whole range of possible or desirable learning outcomes.

Nor is the charge that behaviorists are concerned with mere "training" as opposed to "education" entirely fair. Again, it depends on whether the behaviorists will admit that they have carved out a limited domain of the educational enterprise, while insisting that their work deserves attention as at least one way of approaching some fundamental learning problems. The willingness to leave their effort open to the judgment of empirical evaluation, moreover, is often more than can be said for the proposals of some humanists.

What many humanists fear, however, and in some instances these fears are justified, is the naïve acceptance by the public, and by some state legislatures, that the evaluation of teachers and whole school systems should be based upon limited, supposedly measurable behavioral objectives in some kind of "accountability" scheme. It might then be assumed that the teachers, or the schools, or the curriculum and instructional program are exclusively to blame if behavioral objectives are not achieved by a certain percentage of the students, or, even worse, if the objectives of the curricular program are not stated in sufficiently behavioral terminology. The exclusive adoption by the public of both behavioral objectives and behaviorism's limited view of learning can be used as a political lever to exclude more important personal and social goals of the school.

The point of reviewing the competing views of the humanists and the behaviorists is to indicate that both schools do not have to constantly snipe at one another's heels, that both have something to say to each other and can mutually benefit each other by working more closely together.

Another old dispute that still continues involves those who would focus primarily on the individual personal freedom of the student and those who would focus on social adaptation and citizenship. The heavy emphasis by some on individualized instruction, on letting the student choose when and what he will study on the basis of his own interests and curiosity, tends to relegate such social requirements as cooperation with the legal structures and parental authority to the background. Those who argue for social adaptation and the development of good citizenship behavior, on the other hand, can appear to minimize the need for personal freedom of conscience, for affective relationships, and for individual self-actualization.

We can perhaps evaluate the argument by pointing to the philosophical roots of the differing points of view.[7] The personal freedom group (including A. S. Neil, Friedenberg, Goodman, and Reich) favors the philosophical position of Jean Jacques Rousseau. Rousseau, with his "noble savage" concept of man, conceives of man as inherently good, noble, and innocent but as eventually corrupted by society, its rules and regulations, taboos, and neurotic fears, its compromises and hypocritical social roles and mores. If parents, educators, government authorities, and others, would leave children alone, children would naturally develop a healthy sense of affection, trust, compassion, and a sense of justice. Many of these same assumptions appear in the writings of the personal freedom group.

The social adaptation group (including Broudy, Stanley, Hutchins, Rickover, and Donald Barr) seems to favor the philosophical position of Thomas Hobbes. Hobbes saw man as inherently selfish and aggressive. In order for men to live together in society with some kind of order and peace, individuals had to surrender, through a social contract, some of their own freedoms to the state so that they in return could be protected from exploitation at the hands of others. Although not this explicit, the social adaptation group seems to assume that society has the right to expect schools to indoctrinate youth into the requirements of adult life, to channel them into socially productive work roles, and to condition them for the responsibilities of parenthood, voting, material consumption, and middle-class social behavior.

As an observer of actual practice in large public junior and senior high schools, I often witness this conflict. The social system of the school, with its sanctions, discipline, rewards, rules and regulations, legal and professional authority system, which some have called the hidden curriculum, is thoroughly Hobbesian in tenor, while the curriculum instruction system is often primarily, though implicitly, based on Rousseau's image of man. Usually the social system within the school completely undermines whatever impact the curriculum might have in developing curiosity and free inquiry. Students grow cynical about teacher exhortations of creativity and autonomy when they are forced to request a pass to go to the bathroom.

Ironically enough, we find someone like Jonathan Kozol bitterly criticizing the romantics who would follow A. S. Neil in their efforts to promote freedom and spontaneity in youth. He does not disagree that these are ideals which in an ideal world would be worthwhile; rather, he claims that summerhill-type schools are havens for the spoiled children of the wealthy, who do not have to face up to the harsh reality of an oppressive environment. Kozol's type of "free school," on the contrary, would provide a strict and demanding environment, for that is the only way the children of the poor can be toughened and trained to deal politically with the discriminatory use of power against them.

While I would side with the instincts of those who consider individual human growth toward freedom to be the central emphasis of the curriculum and organizational setting of the school, I, too, am wary of the upper-middle-class bias and of the value neutrality that runs through the writing of many in the personal freedom group. It seems to me, for example, that one of the shortcomings of Silberman's work is that he glorifies schools in Newton, Massachusetts, and other wealthy suburbs where the youth are already assured of a comfortable future. Where does the realistic confrontation with life's harsher realities enter into their experience? An all-pervasive experience of adult life, whether in the home, in community politics, or on the job, is conflict resolution. Another such experience involves the confrontation of social, economic, and political structures—taxation systems, licensing and accrediting systems in education, zoning regulations, and so forth—that inhibit the full exercise of freedom. These structures are not going to evaporate, as Charles Reich seems to suggest, if I simply change from consciousness II to consciousness III and adapt my life style. I would prefer to live and act from a consciousness III level, but I keep bumping into structural elements that pervade the society I live in, which will not yield to a smile, an offering of flowers, or a Bob Dylan song.

The point I'd like to make is that the education-for-ecstasy people, the schools-without-failure people appear to speak from an upper-middle-class, utopian bias and fail to recognize that the exercise of freedom requires constant political negotiation. There is a kind of Heisenberg principle operative in society, namely, that, to ensure the basic freedoms of individuals, laws, sanctions, and institutions must be established which, by their nature, demand that the individual negotiate his behavior according to their rules and not according to spontaneous desire. As Schwab cogently remarks,

a curriculum based on a theory about individual personality which thrusts society, its demands, and its structure far into the background or which ignores them entirely can be nothing but incomplete and doctrinaire, for the individuals in question are in fact members of a society and must meet its demands to some minimal degree since their existence and prosperity as individuals depend on the functioning of society.[8]

It is possible to agree with the individual freedom group's criticism of the misuse of authority, power, and laws in education without accepting the abolition of authority, power, and law. Reform, yes; deschooling, no.

While I would caution against an exclusive concentration on individualized personal growth to the neglect of the complementary social adaptation orientation, I would agree with Harold Shane[9] that what is presented in the literature as teaching the democratic process reflects the folklore of democracy, not its reality as it is practiced in this country. Such naïveté among theoreticians receives support from social theorists, among them Talcott Parsons and his followers, who assume a basic rationality in their analysis of social dynamics.[10] Parsons seems to assume that decision making follows the logic of scientific method and technological efficiency, and that social change takes place primarily in a rational fashion.

A wholly different perspective of social change and the art of politics derives from viewing it through the conflict model, however. From this vantage point, change only occurs when those who have less power aggressively confront those who have more power and wrest some of it from them.[11] In our country, moreover, the con-

crete practices of our capitalistic system seem to dominate government and politics much more than the ideology of egalitarian democracy. Many Americans are constantly engaged in power trade-offs, in
a highly competitive quest for personal gain. They will use every
political trick to attain those ends—egalitarianism be damned. Ask
the Blacks, Chicanos, Indians, and Puerto Ricans what democracy
means to them, and they will tell you that it is the pious rhetoric
used by whites to cloak their ruthless opposition to increased political and economic equality for minorities.

The social adaptation goals of education, therefore, must strive for
an honest appraisal of how capitalism has in fact distorted the democratic ideals of this country, and of the need for constant reformation of the political process to protect the rights of all segments of
our society. The personal freedom group seldom alludes to the need
for young adults to act responsibly as citizens, to promote the welfare of all members of the community, to engage in a continuous
reform of the political process. The wealthy, perhaps, can withdraw
into a private world to tend to their health gardens and other frivoli-
ties, but, if this country is to maintain any kind of character, we
cannot allow a silent and passive majority of citizens to withdraw
from active participation in the political process. As a practicing high
school principal, I am appalled by my students' lack of awareness of
their political responsibilities. They can quote Marcuse, Roszak, and
Reich, but they do not give a practical damn about getting in and
mixing it up in the political arena to make this a better world for
others.

Again, the point of emphasizing this controversy between these
two groups is to indicate that the last word has not been spoken on
the ways of striking a balance between individual personal growth
and social and political awareness and concern as foci for curriculum
theory and practice.[12]

A third major conflict among curriculum theorists involves academicians and moralists. Academicians tend to come from within the
classical liberal arts tradition, and they would promote hard-headed,
intellectual rigor, logical rationality, and concentration on the traditional disciplines such as the natural and social sciences and the
humanities. Moralists claim that education's primary task is to build
character and maturity, to build virtuous and healthy men and wom-
en, and that schools should, therefore, engage students by example

and by practice in efforts to clarify and appreciate values, to develop heroes and altruistic attitudes, and to accept responsibility in their personal and public lives.

The academicians have always found champions among college and university professors, from the Committee of 19 to the promoters of the "structures of the disciplines" of the last decade. People like the great headmasters of the private prep schools (from Boyden to Donald Barr), as well as progressive educators of the twenties and thirties who talked about "educating the whole child," and, more currently, people like Carl Rogers or Arthur Foshay or Lawrence Kubie could broadly be considered in the moralist school. To make their point about the questionable, exclusive concentration on academic disciplines, the moralists point to what Kubie calls "the idiot-savant, a man who is a scholar in his field, but humanly speaking an ignoramus . . ."[13] The academicians counter that they are not baby-sitters, hand holders, or amateur counselors; the primary purpose of schooling is to develop the mind and an appreciation for man's achievements in the scholarly and cultural fields; let parents, psychologists, and clergymen look to the moral development of youth. Foshay seems to strike a healthy balance in his recent curriculum proposals for the 1970's, although he does seem to promote a naïve concept of democracy based on the folklore of democracy mentioned earlier.[14]

There are, to be sure, other disputes, controversies, and opposing theoretical positions in this field, for curriculum theorists display about as much ideological diversity as present-day Jesuits. The three mentioned above seem important here because it remains to be seen whether, in subsequent discussions, we can find a theory to unify and organically relate these points of view in a more comprehensive framework, or whether, based on a wholly different set of ideas the critical importance of which may point to a totally new effort, these controversies may appear nugatory or frivolous.

CHALLENGE

Since we are dealing with the present state of curriculum theory, I would next like to address a serious challenge to the whole field. Joseph Schwab in 1969 urged us to divert our efforts from curriculum theory toward "the Practical" and its manifold pragmatic problems. [15] Since Professor Schwab is among the most respected men in the field of curriculum, this proposal caused more than a stir within curriculum circles. His criticism of the one-sidedness of many theoretical curriculum positions, some of which we have highlighted above, was quite to the point. His direct and caustic impatience with the inability of curriculum theory to make much difference in classroom practice and student learning was refreshing. And I think his foot stamping and table pounding did the field a lot of good. There were too many of us wearing our own version of the Emperor's New Clothes, captivated by our own vision and oblivious to some of the clamoring needs of students and teachers.

Having said that, I must take issue with Schwab's conclusion that we ought to call a moratorium on theoretical speculation and devote our attention to dealing with more practical affairs, like the maintenance and improvement of existing institutions and practices. He also suggested an eclectic use of a variety of theories when they suit the purpose of improving praxis in a specific situation or a specific school.

Schwab's highlighting of the fragmentation of theory points to the lack of a sufficiently comprehensive philosophy of man and society from which to draw comprehensive theoretical curriculum positions. In part, that is the fault of colleges and graduate schools of education in which philosophical inquiry amounts to little more than a survey of the history of philosophy or an exercise in linguistic analysis. [16] Logical positivism—namely, that only empirically quantifiable and measurable matters will yield truth—appears to be a basic cultural bias in our society. This has largely been responsible for a decline in philosophical inquiry during the last two generations, with the result that the younger generation of those involved in curriculum theory have little more than a patchwork of rather vague philosophical assumptions about man and society to stand behind their theoretical positions in curriculum. In short, we appear to have no great philosophers available to us today, no one of the stature and breadth of vision of John Dewey, John Stuart Mill, William James, Alfred North Whitehead, Hegel, Schelling, Locke, Aquinas. A Paulo Freire or a Teilhard de Chardin offers fresh philosophical insights but not a sufficiently comprehensive analysis to integrate the variety and complexity of contemporary human and natural phenomena into a meaningful whole.

Schwab's documentation of the incompleteness of contemporary theory leads him to recommend a moratorium on theory. It leads me to the opposite recommendation: namely, that at least some of our universities should promote and cultivate a vigorous revival of philosophical inquiry in an attempt to go beyond the meticulous commentaries on previous philosophers. We need, perhaps, a brief moratorium on the excessive and nugatory publication of philosophical essays so that young philosophers will have time to study and reflect without the incessant pressure to get something, however premature and inconsequential, into print. What our society, as well as our educators, need is more stimulation to reflect upon the nature of man and society so that they can perceive the underlying significance inside of the confusing circus of daily experiences they face. The one-dimensional and fragmented theory we suffer with at present seems to require a much larger effort to develop a comprehensive theory, rather than a need to flee the task of theory in despair and immerse ourselves in the perhaps more satisfying but shortsighted tasks of solving immediate problems.

My second criticism of Schwab's position is that he confuses roles. His recommendation that curriculum scholars move into the arena of pragmatic problem solving in the schools, or that curriculum scholars conduct much more empirical research on what actually goes on in the classroom is like recommending that architects leave their drawing boards, take up hammer and saw, and deal with the practical problems of carpenters, construction foremen, or the building contractor himself. The political negotiation and management of educational programs is the job of teachers, administrators, and central office supervisors, not of curriculum theorists. They may and should be consulted, but they should not be called on to perform the tasks of front-line personnel. And empirical research on classroom interaction, such as is being conducted by Arno Bellack or by Bunnie Smith, while useful and informative, cannot by itself result in normative or prescriptive theories of curriculum and instruction. Rather, whatever judgments might flow from their descriptions would be tied to prior theoretical assumptions.

The eclectic sorting out of useful ideas for limited educational goals, which is another of Schwab's suggestions, is most profitably accomplished by front-line personnel. President Bok, in his recent annual report to the Harvard University community, seems to be attempting to implement a variety of approaches to undergraduate liberal education.[17] Here is a good example of an administrator attempting to work out with his faculty the pragmatic details of meeting a variety of educational needs of students. From personal observation and through reports it appears that elementary and secondary school principals, department chairmen, and central office supervisors have, in fact, come up with increasingly multiform designs that seem more adequately to meet the multiform needs of their students. Teachers are continually picking and choosing from a variety of curricular materials to find the best instructional fit for their classes.

If, as Schwab seems to suggest, curriculum theorists were to engage in these practical problems, they would almost certainly have to leave their posts in the university, go into the schools, and stay with the day-to-day pragmatic and political management of the instructional program. They cannot realistically accomplish the tasks of "the Practical" from their offices in the university.

I speak from experience, for I left the university to go into a high school and engage in such front-line reform and improvement. The cultural shock was severe. I realized, after the first few days, that most of my time had to be devoted to the daily problems of political negotiation with parents, faculty, and students, not to mention financial auditors. I also realized, on the other hand, my need for stimulation from my former colleagues in curriculum theory to broaden my vision, to look at alternative approaches, to discover lacunae in my own pragmatic program planning and management. But I knew that my colleagues in the university could not map out all the logistical, financial, and political decisions for me; that had to be done on the job.

If curriculum theorists, then, were to follow Schwab's suggestion wholeheartedly, they would cease to be theorists and would become administrators, central office programmers, or teachers. While that might be a salutary experience for many curriculum theorists, it would result in the disappearance of the field of curriculum theory, at least until its place was absorbed by some other group. And I don't think Schwab would go that far. It seems, however, that either one is going to be a theorist or a practitioner. Occupying some middle position, as Schwab seems to suggest, just will not work; the resulting recommendations would suffer from all the defects, and more, that Schwab claims current curriculum theory now reflects.

A third objection to Schwab's position relates to his proposal that curriculum theory focus on present educational institutions and practices and cease plotting schemes for entirely new and wholly different schools. In so far as curriculum theory is involved with utopian proposals, with little appreciation of the political arena in which such utopian proposals would get chopped to pieces, he is right on target. On the other hand, besides confusing the roles of theoretician and practitioner, his suggestion could be dangerously shortsighted. When one becomes engaged in identifying and repairing frictions and failures in the school organization and programs, it tends to absorb all of one's attention. To abandon the task of farsighted speculation would be similar to an automobile company that engages all of its energies in developing a pollution-free gasoline engine and cannot foresee that there will not be enough gasoline to continue to fuel its automobiles beyond ten years.

One of the ongoing tasks of the curriculum theorist is to clarify the meaning of functional literacy, "life skills,"[18] or survival skills.[19] The practitioner whose immersion in the immediate task of keeping the ship afloat has little time to engage in frontier research or future-oriented speculation about what skills students will need to cope with the demands of the immediate future. While the harried practitioner can get some stimulation from authors like Toffler, he needs people in curriculum theory to help him see the educational implications of Toffler's exposition. Were curriculum theorists to abandon their proper role and engage in the practical problems of maintenance and incremental institutional reform, schools could blindly drift into obsolescence at a time when our planetary survival may depend on the development of a whole new set of cultural attitudes and a different sense of national purpose.

While acknowledging the accuracy of Schwab's criticism of the many shortcomings in curriculum theories, I strongly oppose his recommendation that curriculum theorists abandon theory and divert their efforts to the realm of the practical. On the contrary, his critical analysis of the limitations of current theory should spur efforts to develop a more comprehensive and realistic philosophy of man and society, which would then provide a framework for developing more comprehensive curriculum theory.

FUTURE CONCERNS

Finally, this overview might be incomplete unless we asked ourselves whether the current state of curriculum theory is neglecting
any area of major importance. Just this year the Association for
Supervision and Curriculum Development devoted its yearbook to
education for peace.[20] Only a few months ago, *Phi Delta Kappan*
published a special essay by Harold Shane, which highlighted the
need for future-oriented knowledge and survival skills in the light of
the global crises of population explosion, pollution of the biosphere,
threat of nuclear war, and the growing economic imbalance between
developed and developing nations.[21] Just last year, the National
Catholic Education Association announced a new department devoted to developing peace curricula. These recent efforts, as well as
occasional essays in the literature, are beginning to address what has
been seriously neglected: namely, concern for the global community
and its survival, preservation, and development. It remains to be seen
whether these recent expressions of concern will grow into the all-
encompassing concern of a large segment of the curriculum field for
the next decade or so.

In one of the most penetrating essays on the "macroproblem" of
the global crisis, Willis Harman of the Stanford Research Institute
writes:

In view of the world macroproblem, the foremost educational need is to train in
ecological thinking and appreciation of human diversity from the primary
grades. At all levels there is a need for a holistic, future-oriented, transdisciplin-
ary, problem-centered, change-oriented study of human problems, for an understanding of complex wholes and historic parallels. Equally needed at all levels is
continuing study, with progressively more sophisticated conceptual tools, of the
broad human questions of justice and equality of opportunity, of individual
liberty to seek fulfillment, of local and world community, and of human dignity.[22]

The crisis, or the global macroproblem, is developing from many
interrelated global problems[23] that, taken cumulatively, pose a radical threat to man's survival. Among these global problems we can list
the following: overpopulation; exhaustion of the world's energy resources; pollution of the biosphere; the threat of global extermina-
tion by nuclear weapons; unjust relationships and dehumanizing
structures in the political, economic, social, and technological areas

within and between nations; the rapidly widening gap between wealthy nations and third-world countries. The causes of many of these global problems appear to be due not so much to a basic malice among men, but more to an accumulation of relatively well-intentioned, compartmentalized decisions based primarily on economic and technological values, rather than on human values.

Historically, Western man's inclination to make these kinds of decisions stems from the classical economic point of view that, through the law of open-market competition, individuals (and corporations, cities, and countries) could make decisions based on enlightened self-interest, which, taken cumulatively, would result in the common good. The classical model would look like the following:

$$\text{microdecision}_1 + \text{microdecision}_2 + \ldots \text{microdecision}_n = \text{MACROGOOD}$$

This theory assumed that there would be cumulative rationality to a lot of separate and self-interest decisions, resembling the law of natural selection in biological evolution. To some, it was also an expressed, survival of the fittest approach to economic and political affairs.

Behind the values that motivated compartmentalized or microdecisions was a network of assumptions about man, his work, the nature of society, and other aspects of life, which Harman summarizes in a paradigm:

Industrial State Paradigm

1. The premise that the pride of families, the power of nations, and the survival of the human species all are to be furthered (as in the past) by population increase.
2. The "technological imperative" that any technology that can be developed, and any knowledge that can be applied, should be.
3. The premise that the summed knowledge of experts constitutes wisdom.
4. The reductionist view of man, a premise associated with the development of contemporary natural and social sciences, that lends sanction to dehumanizing ways of thinking about and treating man.
5. The premise that man is separate from nature, and hence that nature is to be exploited and controlled rather than cooperated with.
6. The "economic man" image, leading to a system of economics based on ever-increasing GNP, consumption, and expenditures of irreplaceable resources.
7. The premise that the future of the planet can safely be left to autonomous nation-states.

8. The disbelief that "what ought to be" is a meaningful concept and is achievable.[24]

These basic premises have governed many of the political, economic, and social decisions of Western man since the Reformation and the Enlightenment.

Today, even scientists and economists are beginning to see that the unanticipated consequences of technological invention, industrial capitalism, and economic trade relationships have become so dysfunctional, dehumanizing, and destructive that we can no longer avoid looking at the resulting global problems and judging the cumulative effects of smaller microdecisions on them. Widespread pollution of lakes, rivers, and the ocean is an example of a global problem affected by many separate microdecisions of cities and countries relative to dumping human and industrial waste.

This suggests a whole new way of reaching decisions about the present and the future, namely, that we give primary attention to global decisions in the light of these larger problems. Because man's future is in doubt, we need to think about man's survival, not simply the survival of a person, a family, or a country, because their survival hinges on a shared concern for mankind's survival. The beginning of a solution to the global crisis is to recognize that we cannot ignore it while tending to business as usual. The next step is to see that solutions to global problems occupy the foreground of educational effort.

This leads to the question of which values will provide a base and a measure for global or macrosolutions. By the testimony of some economists and technologists, these values must come from beyond the strict realm of economics and technology; they must, in fact, come from humanistic values, such as honesty, integrity, cooperation, responsibility, justice, caring, self-fulfillment, joy. If the only way to solve global problems is through decisions based on humane values, then these values are not only moral imperatives but functional imperatives.

Harman has proposed what he feels are emerging shifts in basic attitudes that would permit humane values to become more functional and normative.

Characteristics of an Emerging Human Paradigm

1. The complementarity of physical and spiritual experience; recognition of all "explanation" as only metaphor; use of different, noncontradicting "levels of explanation" for physical, biological, mental, and spiritual reality.
2. The teleological sense of life; evolution having direction and purpose; ultimate reality perceived as unitary, with transcendent order.
3. The basis for value postulates discoverable in one's own inner experience of a hierarchy as well as a subconscious influence.
4. An articulation of life goals through conscious participation in individual growth and the evolutionary process; individual fulfillment through community; integration of work, play, and growth.
5. An articulation of social goals: to foster development of individuals' transcendent and emergent potentialities. Economic growth, technological development, design of work roles and environments, authority structures, and social institutions all are to be used in the service of this primary goal.
6. The rediscovery of naturalism, holism, supernatural, the politics of consciousness.[25]

What seems to be becoming dramatically evident is that humane values, which have been thought of as an added luxury to the "real" business of competing for a living, are now seen to be a prerequisite basis and guide for economic, political, and technological decisions. And this is being said by economists, businessmen, politicians, and technologists, men not always known for their public piety and altruism. Instead of saying, "Survival in order to be human," they are now saying, "We must be human in order to survive."

Although the Association for Supervision and Curriculum Development has done the curriculum field a real service in its current yearbook, much more remains to be done. Curriculum theorists have a huge task ahead of them: to describe the varieties of human knowledge and experience that will promote the development of personal, sociopolitical, and academic skills necessary to cope with the global challenge. In the speculation and theory yet to come, the development of heightened consciousness must be one of the critical components of any new curriculum proposals. Cultural Revolution? If that is not what we have been talking about when we call for the changes in our national consciousness and our sense of national purpose that are required to meet the global crisis, then I do not know what the term means.

NOTES

1. Louise Tyler, *A Selected Guide to Curriculum Literature: An Annotated Bibliography* (Washington, D. C.: Center for the Study of Instruction, National Education Association, 1970).

2. Curriculum Service Center, National Association of Secondary School Principals, *Curriculum Report* 2, no. 3 (March 1973).

3. Joseph J. Schwab, *The Practical: A Language for Curriculum* (Washington, D. C.: The Center for the Study of Instruction, National Education Association, 1970).

4. Thomas J. Sergiovanni and Robert J. Starratt, *Emerging Patterns of Supervision: Human Perspectives* (New York: McGraw-Hill Book Company, 1971), ch. 11.

5. James B. Macdonald, "Myths about Instruction," *Educational Leadership* 22, no. 8 (May 1965), 571-76, 609-17.

6. Benjamin S. Bloom, "An Introduction to Mastery Learning Theory," paper read to the AERA Symposium, "Schools, Society, and Mastery Learning," held on 28 February 1973, at New Orleans, as part of the Proceedings of the AERA annual meeting. Cf. also James H. Block, ed., *Mastery Learning: Theory and Practice* (New York: Holt, Rinehart and Winston, Inc., 1971).

7. By lumping the people mentioned below together in this somewhat arbitrary grouping, we are obviously overlooking the many and varied nuances of their positions. We do so only to emphasize, perhaps by overstatement, the differences in the positions. Regarding the philosophical positions, see John E. Longhurst, *Essay on Comparative Totalitarianisms: The Twin Utopias of Hobbes and Rousseau* (Lawrence, Kansas: Coronado Press, 1966).

8. Schwab, *The Practical*, p. 23.

9. Harold G. Shane, "Looking to the Future: Reassessment of Educational Issues of the 1970's," *Phi Delta Kappan* 54, no. 5 (January 1973), 332.

10. Talcott Parsons, *Essays in Sociological Theory* (New York: The Macmillan Company, 1954).

11. Cf. Ralph Dahrendorf, *Class and Class Conflict in Industrial Society* (Palo Alto, Calif.: Stanford University Press, 1959); Paulo Freire, *Pedagogy of the Oppressed* (New York: Herder and Herder, 1970).

12. An excellent theoretical treatment of the controversy was done by Vivian S. Sherman, *Two Contrasting Educational Models: Applications and Policy Implications* (Menlo Park, California: Stanford Research Institute, 1970). Sherman not only analyzes the elements of an open and structured educational program, but offers an action research model for various attempts to integrate the strengths of each perspective.

13. Lawrence S. Kubie, "Research in Protecting Preconscious Functions in Education," in Harry Passow, ed., *Nurturing Individual Potential* (Washington, D. C.: Association for Supervision and Curriculum Development, 1964), p. 31.

14. Arthur W. Foshay, *Curriculum for the 50's: An Agenda for Invention* (Washington, D. C.: Center for the Study of Instruction, National Education Association, 1970).

15. Schwab, *The Practical.*

16. Cf. Sherman, *Two Contrasting Educational Models*, pp. 2-3, where she underlines the need for much greater clarity for the philosophical assumptions underlying educational positions and practices.

17. Derek C. Bok, "The President's Report," *Harvard Today* (March 1973), 7-12.

18. Cf. Louis J. Rubin, ed., *Life Skills in School and Society* (Washington, D. C.: Association for Supervision and Curriculum Development, 1969), p. 23: "When we ponder the skills most needed, we must not fail to attend to the capacities which breed social awareness and social concern, and we must not overlook those skills which enable one to judge what is worthwhile in life and what is not." See also Alexander Frasier, "Individualized Instruction," *Educational Leadership* 25, no. 1 (April 1968), 616-24, in which Frasier underlines the need to develop in youth the power of enjoyment, sensibility, invention, endurance, and love, besides the traditional academic skills; see also, Kimbal Wiles, "Values and Our Destiny," in Robert R. Leeper, ed., *Curricular Concerns in a Revolutionary Era* (Washington, D. C.: Association for Supervision and Curriculum Development, 1971), pp. 6-10.

19. Cf. Harold G. Shane, "Looking to the Future"; Alvin Toffler, *Future Shock* (New York: Random House, 1970); Willis W. Harman, *Alternative Futures and Educational Policy* (Menlo Park, California: Stanford Research Institute, 1970); Robert H. Anderson, Millie Almys, Harold G. Shane, and Ralph Tyler, *Education in Anticipation of Tomorrow* (Worthington, Ohio: Charles A. Jones, 1973); D. H. Meadows *et al.*, *The Limits to Growth* (New York: Universe Books, 1972); Jesuit Secondary Education Association, *The Jesuit High School of the Future* (Washington, D. C.: JSEA, 1972).

20. George Henderson, ed., *Education for Peace: Focus on Mankind* (Washington, D. C.: Association for Supervision and Curriculum Development, 1973).

21. Shane, "Looking to the Future."

22. Harman, *Alternative Futures*, p. 17.

23. Cf. Barbara Ward, Rene Dubos, *Only One Earth: The Care and Maintenance of a Small Planet* (New York: W. W. Norton, 1972); Harvey Wheeler, *Democracy in a Revolutionary Era* (Santa Barbara, California: The Center for the Study of Democratic Institutions, 1968), esp. ch. 8, "World Order"; Meadows *et al.*, *Limits to Growth.*

24. Harman, *Alternative Futures*, pp. 9-10.

25. Willis W. Harman, "A Look At Business in 1990," an address given to the White House Conference on the Industrial World Ahead, February 1972.

SELECTED REFERENCES

Anderson, Robert H. (ed.). *Education in Anticipation of Tomorrow* (Worthington, Ohio: Charles A. Jones Publishing Company, 1973).

Block, James H. (ed.). *Mastery Learning: Theory and Practice* (New York: Holt, Rinehart and Winston, Inc., 1971).

Bloom, Benjamin S. "Mastery Learning and Its Implications for Curriculum Development," in Eliot W. Eisner (ed.), *Confronting Curriculum Reform* (Boston: Little, Brown and Company, 1971).

Bok, Derek C. "The President's Report," 1971-72, *Harvard Today* (March 1973).

Bruner, James S. "Needed: A Theory of Instruction," in Leeper, Robert R. (ed.), *Curricular Concerns in a Revolutionary Era* (Washington, D. C.: Association for Supervision and Curriculum Development, 1971).

Chase, John B., and J. Minor Gwynn. *Curriculum Principles and Social Trends* (London: Collier-Macmillan, Ltd., 1969).

Foshay, Arthur W. *Curriculum for the 70's: An Agenda for Invention* (Washington, D. C.: Center for the Study of Instruction, National Education Association, 1970).

Frazier, Alexander. "The Larger Question: A New Sense of Common Identity," in Robert R. Leeper (ed.), *Curricular Concerns in a Revolutionary Era* (Washington, D. C.: Association for Supervision and Curriculum Development, 1971).

Freire, Paulo. *The Pedagogy of the Oppressed* (New York: Herder and Herder, Inc. 1970).

Glasser, William. *Schools without Failure* (New York: Harper and Row Publishers, 1969).

Greene, Maxine. "The Arts in a Global Village," in Robert R. Leeper (ed.), *Curricular Concerns in a Revolutionary Era* (Washington, D. C.: Association for Supervision and Curriculum Development, 1971).

Gutierrez, Gustavo. *A Theory of Liberation* (New York: Maryknoll, 1973).

Harman, Willis W. *Alternative Futures and Educational Policy* (Menlo Park, California: Stanford Research Institute, Research Memorandum, EPRC 6747-6, 1970).

Henderson, George (ed.). *Education for Peace: Focus on Mankind* (Washington, D. C.: Association for Supervision and Curriculum Development, 1973).

Huebner, Dwayne. "Implications of Psychological Thought for the Curriculum," in Glenys G. Unruh and Robert R. Leeper (eds.), *Influences in Curriculum Change* (Washington, D. C.: Association for Supervision and Curriculum Development, 1970).

Jones, Richard M. *Fantasy and Feeling in Education* (New York: New York University Press, 1968).

Kohlberg, Lawrence. "The Moral Atmosphere of the School," in Norman V. Overly (ed.), *The Unstudied Curriculum: Its Impact on Children* (Washington, D. C.: Association for Supervision and Curriculum Development, 1970).

Kozol, Jonathan. *Free School* (Boston: Houghton Mifflin Company, 1972).

Kubie, Lawrence S. "Research in Protecting Preconscious Functions in Education," Harry Passow (ed.), *Nurturing Individual Potential* (Washington, D. C.: Association for Supervision and Curriculum Development, 1964).

Lawrence, Gordon. "Bruner: Instructional Theory or Curriculum Theory?" *Theory in Practice* VIII, No. 1 (February 1969).

Leeper, Robert R. (ed.). *Curricular Concerns in a Revolutionary Era* (Washington, D. C.: Association for Supervision and Curriculum Development, 1971).

Longhurst, John C. *An Essay on Comparative Totalitarianisms: The Twin Utopias of Hobbes and Rousseau* (Lawrence, Kansas: The Coronado Press, 1966).

Macdonald, James B. "Myths About Instruction," in Robert R. Leeper (ed.), *Curricular Concerns in a Revolutionary Era* (Washington, D. C.: Association for Supervision and Curriculum Development, 1971).

Meadows, Donella H., Dennis L. Meadows, *et al. The Limits to Growth* (New York: Universe Books, 1972).

Miller, Bernard S. *The Humanities Approach to the Modern Secondary School Curriculum* (New York: The Center for Applied Research in Education, Inc., 1972).

National Association for Secondary School Principals. *Curriculum Report,* Curriculum Service Center II, No. 3 (March 1973).

Olson, Paul A., Larry Freeman, and James Bowman. *Education for 1984 and After* (Lincoln, Nebraska: Nebraska Curriculum Development Center, University of Nebraska, 1972).

Phi Delta Kappan, *Alternative Schools* LIV, No. 5 (January 1973).

Reich, Charles A. *The Greening of America* (New York: Random House, 1970).

Rubin, Louis J. (ed.). *Life Skills in School and Society* (Washington, D. C.: Association for Supervision and Curriculum Development, 1969).

Schwab, Joseph. *The Practical: A Language for Curriculum* (Washington, D. C.: Center for the Study of Instruction, National Education Association, 1970).

Scriven, Michael. "Education for Survival," G. Kenley (ed.), *The Ideal School* (Wilmette, Illinois: The Kagg Press, 1969).

Shane, Harold G. "Looking to the Future: Reassessment of Educational Issues of the 1970's," *Phi Delta Kappan* LIV, No. 5 (January 1973).

Shane, Harold G. "The Rediscovery of Purpose in Education," in Robert R. Leeper (ed.), *Curricular Concerns in a Revolutionary Era* (Washington, D. C.: Association for Supervision and Curriculum Development, 1971).

Sherman, Vivian S. *Two Contrasting Educational Models: Applications and Policy Implications* (Menlo Park, California: Stanford Research Institute, 1970).

Silberman, Charles E. *Crisis in the Classroom* (New York: Random House, 1970).

Tyler, Louise. *A Selected Guide to Curriculum Literature: An Annotated Bibliography* (Washington, D. C.: Center for the Study of Instruction, National Education Association, 1970).

III. TOWARD A REMAKING
OF CURRICULAR LANGUAGE

Dwayne Huebner

The institutions of education are so pervasive and the problems raised by these institutions are so pressing that to escape from their everydayness is nearly impossible. The danger to an educator, or a would-be educator, is that he will be socialized into the existing institutions or into the language generated by them. One cannot be socially critical as a positivist. That which is, a consequence of historical conditions that may not exist today, is not necessarily what should or could be. To answer questions derived from dated institutions or framed by limited ways of speaking is to limit the imagination and the future. To honor a question does not entail answering the question, but responding to the situation that is the source of the question. To honor an institution or the people associated with an institution does not require maintaining the institution or the behavior of the people; instead, it is an articulation of the time and place of their origin, the time and place of today, and the discrepancies or contradictions that prevail between the two times and the two places. We do not honor educators, their language, and their institutions by accepting at face value the concerns and problems that they generate. We honor them by indicating how these concerns derive from historical commitments and how these problems are a consequence of new technical and political conditions. In the everyday talk of educators, the phenomena of education have been too closely associated with the institutions of schooling and the language of learning. Schools are a necessary social construction, and learning is a necessary intellectual construct. In discussing education, we should not be limited to these two constructs; nor should our discussion ignore them.

My previous work has been an effort to attend to the phenomena of education without being unduly and perhaps unconsciously socialized to the language, the institutions, and the norms of everyday educators. I think that I can now penetrate the realities that the everyday educator takes for granted, and I can illuminate what he is about in such a way that his own concerns and the complexities of the age can be more clearly seen and acted upon. I intend to articulate the phenomena of education in such a way that school people can see what they are about and nonschool people can envision other possibilities. In so doing I intend, eventually, to provide a language that can reveal how the educator has decided to live in the world and what he sees as possible futures.

In "Education as Concern for Man's Temporality," I pointed to education as concern for the evolving biography of the person and the evolving history of societies or communities, and I stated that the task of the curriculum person was to think through the dialectical relationships between the individual and the society or community in such a way that both maintained some kind of rhythmic continuity and change. Since the writing of that paper, I have become aware of three facets of man's temporality that facilitate the discussion of intentional education. The first is the phenomena of memory and traditions as these store and make accessible the past. The second is the activity of interpretation, the hermeneutical art, which is the bridge between self and other; a linkage among past, present, and future; the vehicle by which individuals, in community, arrive at mutual understanding in the conduct of their public affairs. The third is the phenomenon of community as a caring collectivity in which individuals share memories and intentions.

Everyday usage of the word *education* tends to emphasize the individual. We tend to talk about educating a person. This everyday usage, however, does not correspond to some of the concerns of the educator, who also acts to maintain aspects of the society. The educator too easily speaks of what a child "must learn." He does so, not necessarily because he cares for the child, but because he is concerned that certain aspects of our society be upheld or maintained. The conflict between the "needs" of society and the "needs" of children creates tensions that are manifest in problems of control, in guilt over the educator's use of power, and sometimes in a neurotic incapacity to act. The perceptions that are the source of the tension, the guilt, and the inability to act can be modified if the word *education* is used to refer to the futuring of the person and the futuring of a society. If education is talked about as concern for the evolving biography of the person and the evolving history of a community or society, then the phenomenon of power can more easily be lived within. The conflict between the individual and the community becomes a fact of human existence that need not cause neurotic inaction but could create, instead, an awareness of one's freedom to participate in public life. Conflict can free a person to be political, to use power, and to struggle with others over the various manifestations of power. The language of learning and of socialization hides the conflicts, the freedom for political action, the significance of power, and, indeed, the whole temporal nature of man. The languages of human development, political socialization, objectives of education, and therapy tend to hide the problems of community, power, tradition, and temporality and the hermeneutical arts. If the educator is to be conscious of what he is about and how he is to act, then his everyday languages must be rethought and reconstructed.

At birth a child is pushed out, not thrown, into an already established world. The reception he receives in the delivery room and in the maternity ward of the hospital speaks of the world today in the United States in contrast to the world elsewhere. The child is pushed out among people with specific traditions or memories and intentions. Some of these traditions and memories are sedimented in the various institutions and instruments that make up the public world. But they are also sedimented in the way that people, preconsciously, are with others and speak with others. To speak of a child's inheritance at this age can be verbal self-justification of the adult. We want the child to maintain the life style into which he is pushed. To soften that demand, we claim that the child inherits.

We can easily teach the new being to accept our standards, concealing from ourselves the power that we exercise over another in the act of teaching. In the early months this is not as obvious. Care for the new being is easy, and his intrusions into the already established are not too demanding. They may, indeed, be a part of our expectations. But, as the child becomes more demanding, our care for him conflicts with our care for ourselves. We hide the conflict under the language of social necessity.

From the moment of someone else's birth we must scrutinize the language we use to describe what happens to the new being in our midst. We must become aware that our language is reflexive, at least to a knowledgeable observer. It expresses something about us as well as something about the world. In talking about something outside ourself, we also talk about ourself, even if we have not been trained to recognize it. As we talk about the new being among us, we forgetfully take ourselves and our ways for granted, thus unthinkingly shaping the new being into these ways. The language of socialization encourages us to assume that the new being must be brought into near conformity with what we take for granted to be our world. Our language does not encourage us to see him or her as a living question about that which we take for granted. As we condition the new being to our taken-for-granted ways, we hide from our awareness that living together is the sharing of memories and intentions and the building of public, or shared, worlds.

By making these comments about the child as a new being, I do not intend to take a romantic view of the child, nor to make a statement about the goodness of man versus the evil of society. I do intend to call attention to the language for talking about the infant and child that tends to mask the life style of the parent or educator: traditions, memories, and intentions. This language is unconsciously furthered and developed by the scientific study of the child, a study that has ignored the place of the adult in the child's world, the politics of adult-child relationships, the child's participation in the building of public worlds, and the art of interpretation about the meaning of life as people, children, and adults live it together.

The presence of the new being gives rise to one of our concerns in education. That is the concern for transcendence, liberation, emancipation, or however you might wish to speak about temporality of the person. It is the question of how a new being is sheltered in this world, how he is cared for and honored, how he is respected and responded to as creator. It is the question answered by the language of human growth and development, but the uncritical acceptance of this terminology must be questioned.

The presence of the new being is not the only presence which gives rise to educational concern. The public world into which a new being is pushed is already established. Aspects of the natural world have been converted into social goods. The ways in which people have lived together have been converted into certain services. The new being is thrown into the midst of a complexity of goods and services, traditions and embodied memories, and the intentions of those who have lived in this place at another time. These goods and services are manifest in our technologies, and in the economic and political institutions sedimented out over the years. The traditions, memories, and intentions of our predecessors are embodied in the public world and taken for granted. Our collective wealth as a species consists of the embodied traditions, the technologies, and the institutions that now make up the diverse public worlds. Two educational concerns are brought forth by the presence of the past. First, who should have access to what segments of this collective wealth? Second, how should the collective wealth, the memories, and the traditions be maintained and protected from loss or forgetfulness?

The presence of the new being and the presence of the past create tensions where they are together. Without the loving care of people, the traditions embodied in technologies and institutions would decay and return to the earth, no longer a part of the social world but of the natural world. Without the loving care of people, the new being would die and also become part of the natural organic world. Care for the new being, the child, can be inhibited or even prevented by the way in which care for the public world is manifest. If the collective wealth is distributed in certain patterns, for example, if nutrients are not equitably distributed by our technologies, by our economic delivery systems, and by our patterns of political justice, then some children will never be able to participate in the public world. Care for the past can be inhibited by the way in which we care for the new being, for memories, traditions, and collective wealth can be forgotten and disappear from human memory.

The tension between care for the new being and care for collective wealth is lived out in the community and in the struggles among diverse communities. If a community is a group of people with common or shared memories and intentions, then the new being is pushed out, not only into a public world but into an ongoing community with traditions of care for people and traditions of care for collective or public wealth. The Biblical image of people in pilgrimage is what I have in mind. The wayfaring communities carry with them their care for each other and care for their possessions and their memories stored in their poetry, their songs and rituals, their tools, and their other traditions. The presence of a community with traditions of care for people and for collective wealth, a community that honors and develops individual and collective memory, that articulates and acts out intentions is the third fact that gives rise to educational concern. Without education the community could not maintain its pilgrimage beyond a single generation. It would die out along the way and foreclose the rest of the journey. Without education, traditions and memories would be forgotten, hope would be ignored, and futures would remain unclaimed. Without education the new being would be lost and transcendence would be unknown.

I am right where every other educator has been. Nothing is new here, except perhaps some of the terminology used to articulate the place. An educator cannot intentionally educate without thinking about the individual, the society, and the culture or tradition. It is in talk about these three presences and their being together in a place that we clarify our memories, share our intentions, and feel our powers in conflict. It is in talk about these three presences that we find the stuff for our hermeneutical and world-building arts. It is in asking how these three presences have been together in the past that we give direction to historical inquiry. It is in thinking about the togetherness of these three presences that we articulate educational organization and educational method.

Most recently our thinking about these three presences has been governed by talk about the individual. This is not to say that our priority is the individual and that his concerns and feelings, his memories and intentions are uppermost. Rather, it is to say that our language starts with the individual. We ask how he learns, what he should learn, and what materials are necessary if he is to learn. This starting point in our thinking has pushed individual psychology to a position of primacy in educational talk. It has also placed concern for educational material and the quality of school life into a secondary position. I do not wish to displace the individual from a position of primacy in our thinking. I do wish to claim an equal place for the past and for the community. In thinking about education we cannot effectively start our thinking with the individual and then make the past and the community secondary. Rather, our thinking must start with all three: the individual, the past, and the community. Then we can ask how the three are interrelated. We need not relate them by the language of teaching and learning, or by goals and objectives. I suggest that they can be interrelated by hermeneutical or interpretive activity, by political activity, and by work activity.

It seems to me, then, that our curriculum questions should be phrased something like this: What past, that is, what collective memories, traditions, and artifacts can be made present for what child in the presence of what community? What kinds of activity occur among those three presences? By these questions I intend, ultimately, to bring into focal attention the phenomena of subjectivity and intersubjectivity, freedom as participation in a public world, and power. By asking the questions this way, I wish to make explicit the tensions which exist for the would-be educator. He must care for the new being, for the child. What is intended by the expression "care for the new being" will require more elaboration than is possible here, although I will refer to aspects of this care. The educator must also care for the past, conserve it so it will not be forgotten or lost for use and reference. It is this aspect of the educator's task that receives most attention here, but he must also care for the community of which he is a part. This means attending to the memories, intentions, and power of those with whom he dwells; in other words, the educator must seek to be part of a pilgrimage. This concern for community will be alluded to, but not developed directly.

I shall begin with the presence of the past: traditions, memories, and artifacts. Normal educational talk goes like this: We are trying to achieve certain objectives, or to maximize certain values in the behavior of the student. To learn these behaviors, certain materials and adults or teachers with certain skills are needed. How or where can we get them?

What I wish to do is to bracket and remove the steps leading to the selection of the materials and teacher skills and to consider those materials and skills a primary educational good, a manifestation of certain memories, traditions, or artifacts that are to be conserved. Education for reading will provide an example.

Reading is spoken of as a skill—a very complex one made up of many subskills. Our strategy for thinking about education for reading has been something like this: We have identified the components and subcomponents of the reading skills. We have asked ourselves how these various subcomponents are learned and the order in which they should be learned. This has led, in turn, to the production of readers, and, gradually, to the production of workbooks, and, recently, to other diverse material such as kits of self-diagnostic and learning materials, talking typewriters, and other computer-based technologies. Some of these materials are a consequence of psychological theories such as reinforcement theories. During the same period the quantity and quality of literature for young children has increased, by way of paperbacks and the increased number of elementary school libraries. Until about ten years ago the talk about individualizing instruction in reading was primarily that—just talk. The places where such individual instruction was carried out required unusually hardworking teachers who laboriously collected materials, cut up workbooks or developed their own dittoed materials and games. Today the individualization of reading instruction is within the possibility of almost every school, for the marketplace makes available a variety of reading materials. We now have a plurality of methods, a variety of materials, and the lockstep induced by text material has been broken. These developments, except the increase in literature for children, have been brought about by the educator's concern for helping children learn to read and the psychological study of reading processes. It is necessary that we continue to increase our scientific study of the processes of reading, but our concern that young people actually read should not be consumed by scientific methods.

When reading materials did not fit the characteristics of the student population, the educator resorted to three games, predominantly language games: readiness, motivation, and discipline or control. If a child was not "ready" to use the primers or other materials, we talked about readiness and how one developed readiness in the child. If the child was not interested in the materials or the methodology accompanying the materials, we talked about motivation. In fact, when teachers were bound to a single set of readers, a significant segment of the manual for teachers was devoted to motivational exercises, or ways to prepare the children to "receive" the materials. If, after readiness and motivational activity, the materials still did not fit the child, then we had a control problem. Questions of discipline were raised by the teacher. For many, if not most, teachers the problems of teaching reading were primarily discipline or control problems: How do I keep some kids quiet while I work with others, and what do I do with the "slow readers"?

By these comments I intend to call attention to the fact that, when the materials and traditions did not match the child and when the memories and intentions of the educators did not coincide or fit the memories and intentions of the students, power came into play in the guise of manipulative activity. I prefer to call it political activity. The teacher asked how he could impose his subjectivities, memories, intentions, and behaviors on the child. How could the child be brought into the white, middle-class community of the teacher? The use of power, political activity, was necessary because creating a match between child and material was seen as a problem of doing something to the child, not doing something to the public world, not changing the goods or services. In other words, the child was oppressed by the educator because of limited or restricted material and skills, or, in other terms, limited goods and services. The teacher did not serve as the agent of a free individual—the child—but of repressive communities, repressive in part because of limited goods and services. The teacher did not serve as an agent of the child, helping him participate in the continuous reconstruction of the public world, in this case in the continuous reconstruction of the traditions and artifacts of reading. This unconscious choice of agency, the unquestioned use of power, and the denial of the subjectivity of the child for the reaffirmation of the teacher and of those associated with available reading goods and services was the result. It is true, of course, that limited monies and perhaps limited technologies prevented, or presumably prevented, the development of more adequate reading goods and services for a variety of children, including those of different economic classes or communities or with different physiological characteristics. But the influence of the inequitable distribution of public and private wealth was hidden from the educator and the student by the language games of readiness, motivation, and discipline, reinforced by rituals of schooling such as grading, promotion, and the credentials that go with graduation.

In the actions of the student, either as he conforms to or opposes the expectations manifest in the materials and the skills of the educator, and in the actions of the educator as he attempts to overpower the student via readiness, motivational, or disciplining games, we probably find clues to the incipient or actual community to which each belongs. These actions of submission, rebellion, or consent on the part of the student, and love, work, or control on the part of the teacher, are manifestations of the memories and intentions of the communities of which they are a part. More commonly, we would term these values, but that term hides the historical community which is their source. I do not point to this phenomenon with any degree of assurance, but with the suspicion that in the behavior of each we have empirical data to illuminate the nebulous idea of community as it now appears in the educational literature. This idea has increased in importance with the advent of community control.

How else can we articulate what has been happening in this sphere of education known as the teaching of reading? Can we speak of education for reading more directly, using the notion of presences of past, child, and community?

When we speak of reading, we normally speak of what a person does: he reads something to some end. From the perspective of the past, print is a technology in which individual and collective memory, imagery, and intention are made a part of the public world and conserved for others. My use of the word memory is intended to cover theories, stories, and rules or procedures, but the development to that usage would be a long aside. For whom is this past conserved? This question points to those who control print: not simply the writer, but the whole publishing and translating industry, the print distribution systems in the world, and the community traditions of being together and talking together about print. The history of the Bible from manuscript to printed book in Hebrew and Greek, to the Vulgate edition and then into the language idiom of the people via the King James Version and the Revised Standard Version illustrates my intent. The presence of the Bible is often accompanied by other printed materials, such as commentaries or other works of exegetical and hermeneutical arts, along with the oral traditions that accompany the book in diverse communities. At one time access to the printed Bible required command of Hebrew and Greek. Today that no longer applies unless the word Bible is restricted to the earliest Hebrew or Greek texts.

Behind these conserved phenomena of print and print traditions is the educational question: To what extent are they accessible to children three years old, six years old, twelve years old, fifteen years old? To extend the image, what traditions conserved in print are available to the six-year-old child in Appalachia, the Spanish-speaking six-year-old child in Manhattan, the deaf six-year-old child in a school for the handicapped, the six-year-old child in the bush of Uganda? What community traditions accompany the use of these print materials? In our home, my children grow up with books scattered all over the house. They sit next to us while we read silently. We purchase and borrow printed goods for them. We point to the pictures and elaborate in speech, even for the youngest who cannot

yet speak. The children sit next to us as we read and reread stories
and interpret them; we point to words as we say them; we read and
act out *Where the Wild Things Are*. Print is not just something that
we come across; print is something that we put into the world via an
electric typewriter. Even the fifteen-month-old child sits at the typewriter to see what happens to a sheet of paper as she presses keys.
These are communal traditions accompanying print. What communal
traditions are present when the only print present to the child is that
of one textbook in the presence of thirty other like-age children?
What oral reading traditions accompany the textbook in school?
What kind of individual or collective memory, image, or intention is
found in a textbook? How significant are school-bound traditions
when a home embodies no print traditions? How much of the over-
whelming richness of the world is present to the child in the print
available to him?

The question school people ask is: How effectively or efficiently is
reading being taught? I would come back and say that this is a
schooling question, not an educational one. The educational question
is: How is the wealth of, or in, the public world made available to the
child who is six years old, or any other age, and how effective are the
embodied past and its traditions for the same child?

The capability of our society to conserve the stories, images, and
intentions from diverse communities in forms accessible to the young
child has increased significantly. The number of children's writers
and publishers devoted to children's books has increased. Over the
past twenty years, the capability of this economic sector has expanded greatly, and the improvement of reading methodologies in
the schools is but a related effect. Today, the reading textbook is a
severely limited manifestation of this public wealth, and a child who
has access only to a commercial school text is indeed a deprived
child, an economically and technically deprived child. The question,
then, is: How is the print wealth of the world distributed to people
of all ages and all characteristics? What are the vehicles of print
production, translation, distribution? How is private and public
wealth distributed to bring print to the six-year-old child in Appalachia, to the six-year-old deaf child? How are community traditions
that accompany print communicated? Who controls the production
and distribution of print and the communication of traditions that
accompany print? How much does it cost to initiate an adult into the

traditions of oral reading? Into the traditions of caring for print and simultaneously caring for children? How does a society organize politically to adjudicate among those sectors of its technology and economy that produce and distribute pornography for adolescents, delivery systems of word and visual print images for five-year-old children, or napalm delivery systems for Asian children? These questions, which deal with the politics and economics of education, as well as with curriculum, indicate something about the control of schools. They indicate how the narrow concerns for effectiveness, behavioral objectives, and principles of learning have hidden much broader problems of economic and technical policies pertaining to education.

One part of the question of a reading curriculum asks about print and traditions accompanying that print which are available to particular children in particular communities. We can now turn to the other part of the question governing curriculum, namely that of method. When the presence of print and print traditions are brought together with the presence of children and in the presence of particular communities, what activity is possible? Earlier I suggested three forms of activity: hermeneutical, political, and work. By hermeneutical, I intend interpretation; by political, I mean the arriving at agreed upon collective memory and intention or action; by work, I mean the maintaining and building of a public space, a technological consequence of political activity.

I have already alluded to the political activity, which is a consequence of limited material and human skill: control by the educator and the imposition of actions and perhaps intentions and memories. I hope to return to this later. I wish now to attend to what I have called hermeneutical activity, for therein I see a way of getting at pedagogical method and interpreting what goes on in the classroom or other educational places. My source is Palmer's book *Hermeneutics*,[1] although my own introduction to hermeneutics is by way of Heidegger in his many writings, Ricoeur in his work on Freud,[2] and Habermas' *Knowledge and Human Interests*.[3] Palmer traces the word *hermeneutics* back to its Greek source and claims that it "points back to the wingfooted messenger-god Hermes . . . Hermes is associated with the function of transmuting what is beyond human understanding into a form that human intelligence can grasp. The various forms of the word suggest the process of bringing a thing or situation from unintelligibility to understanding" (p. 13). He states that the "Hermes process" is at work when "something foreign, strange, separated in time, space, or experience is made familiar, present, comprehensible: something requiring representation, explanation, or translation is somehow 'brought to understanding'—is interpreted" (p. 14).

It seems to me that the "Hermes Process" as described by Palmer is the pedagogical process, is educational method, at least with respect to education for reading. Thus, in the presence of print, the child is faced with "something foreign, strange, separated in time, space, or experience," and the problem of method is to make it "familiar, present, comprehensible." In this sense, phonetic methods are a form of hermeneutic, of taking the strange symbols in print and making them comprehensible by translating them into sound. I do not wish to pursue this relationship too far for this has the danger of simply substituting the word *hermeneutic* for the words *teaching method*. The significance of the association is that it opens up educational method to new forms of inquiry. Hermeneutics, the art of interpretation, has a long tradition in Western thought. The use of hermeneutics in educational thought could reduce the strain on learning and psychology, thus reserving that body of knowledge and the technology it spawns for more specific and clearly relevant tasks.

Hermeneutical activity is also a tradition carried by communities. The teacher in engaging in instruction, whether by asking questions, establishing written assignments, reading to the child, or pronouncing words for him, is introducing him to traditions of interpretation. The question to be asked is not how the child learns the traditions of interpretation, but how he can dwell in the midst of living traditions and affirm them. I suggest that the various exercises in workbooks and independent skill development activities are forms of interpretational activity, hermeneutical forms, that have been embodied in software rather than in the social relationships between students and teachers. This notion of educational method as a form of hermeneutical activity has been recently opened up to me, and the exploration of its consequences, not only in the education for reading but in education with respect to the past embodied in other forms, is yet to be done.

The scientific study of reading and the technologies that it spawns contribute to the establishment of new traditions and new artifacts.

That is, work activity is associated with education for reading. By establishing new instructional materials and methods, this work activity makes a potential contribution to the public wealth and its conservation in new artifacts and traditions. Since 1920 or so significantly new materials have been brought to children, and new interpretational activities have been initiated between children and adults. Some of these work products are worth conserving and should become part of tradition. This is not true of all of the reading apparatus that has been produced in the past fifty years. Some of the material and methods have been designed as extensions of schools. If schools are seen as manifestations of educational concerns at particular times, and places, now possibly obsolete, then we must be critical of innovations that simply add to the stuff of schools and encourage us to continue to take the schools for granted. By that I do not intend that we should seek to overthrow the school, but, rather, that we should be somewhat certain that new materials and methods have educational meaning, not simply school meaning.

In this concern for conserving the past the question of value is exposed: Is this innovation worthy of becoming part of the collective memory and wealth of a community, of being conserved? If so, is it worthy of being conserved simply as part of the story, an event that did not change the nature of our pilgrimage; or is it a new image, a new instrument that changes significantly the nature of the pilgrimage? The question of value that should be asked in education, then, is not what is valuable and hence should be learned by the young, but what is valuable enough to be conserved as part of the past and made present to the young? By that question I wish to draw attention to the way the educator too frequently talks about learning as a form of normative control rather than as a possibility for the future.

The child, in coming into the presence of print and the communal traditions surrounding or accompanying print, comes up against the public world of others. It is a public world established and maintained through the work and power of writers, editors, publishers, and distributors. It is a world maintained by the work of the child and the teacher within the school. The child must too frequently take that public world for granted, accepting its ready-madeness, perhaps conforming to its demands and requirements. If that ready-made world of print and the communal traditions that accompany it do not fit him, that is, if they do not mesh with his memories and intentions and the Hermes process does not work, then either he is alienated from his own memories and intentions by the power of the teacher or he must withdraw in one way or another from the presence of that formed world. Now, of course, the other option is that he participate in the criticism of that world and seek to establish a better-fitting public world, a world of print and communal traditions surrounding that print that make interpretation possible. This may be in the establishment or development of new forms of interpretational activity via the development of new skills on the part of the teacher, the redevelopment of new skill development software, or the establishment of new stories in print. It may be in the development of other print materials. The young child, however, has too frequently been overpowered by the already existing world and the power of the adult. He has had the incipient political activity of negation and negotiation associated with two- and four-year-old children knocked out of him by adults who see negation as bad. They do not see these negative periods as the establishment of political schemas at a sensory-motor and preoperational level. Hence, the child does not see a misfit as an invitation to rework the public world. He is left with the awareness that the public world is made and that he is a misfit, rather than with the awareness that the public world is always in the process of being reworked and that he has a right to rework it. He does not perceive himself as engaged in work activity or political activity. Hence, he picks up—and becomes a manifestation of and takes on the characteristics of—labels and stereotypes directed at those for whom the public world is a bad fit. However, the slow learner and the handicapped are merely those who do not have the appropriate educational goods and services in their presence. The monies and technologies directed at building the public world of educational goods and services have not been used to build a public world big enough for the educationally disadvantaged—the handicapped, the slow learner. Of course, if monies and technologies are scarce, then it is a problem of economic and political value, a consequence of the distribution of wealth. The production, distribution, and consumption of economic goods influences social relationships in educational places. Given the present distribution of wealth, of money, of technologies, of other values, who indeed is to be disadvantaged, slow, handicapped?

The child is able to participate in work, or at least to see people working to reform the world, in the efforts being made to restructure the public world to better fit those who are in it. To see the teacher actually form her behaviors through videotaping and experimentation and perhaps to participate with her in the study of her own teaching is one example. Another is student participation in the creation of their own software, the writing of their own stories which are then bound into book form and deposited in the school library. Another is serving as an agent of interpretation for a child for whom no present interpretive activity seems to fit. Most desirable, and least accessible presently, is to be tied into the commercial production of print forms via two-way communication channels between schools and publishers. At the present time these are but one-way channels, and teachers and children have only the option to buy and to use or not to use, not the option of participating in the construction of the new forms. Of course, the channel from child to publisher does exist, but indirectly as the publishing industry recognizes new market demands and creates materials to meet these new demands. However, this process could be much more visible and transparent. The existence of a media center in each educational place, which would be responsible for producing educational goods and services or for negotiating with other producers for such production, would be a way of institutionalizing this two-way process.

The school has been seen primarily as a place where the adult community imposes its demands or life styles on the young, or at least as a place where the memories, traditions, and intentions of the adult community are placed in the presence of the young. Everyday usage of school talk, as well as everyday usage of school institutions and instruments, suggests that the learning, the molding, and the forming is of the young by adults. In effect, this means that the child is walled off from public life and participation in that public life as a free agent. By seeing the school as a one-way educational process, from adult to child, and by talking about it as such, the other direction of the process is not seen, the impact of the young on the so-called adult world. In effect, the school serves as a barrier to protect the adult community from the probes, critiques, questions, and doubts of the young. The language of socialization, of course, justifies this barrier, and we proclaim that the young have few rights of participation until socialized. That claim should not stand uncriticized. The school serves as a barrier whereby the world is protected from innocence, from embarrassment by the unsocialized, from shock by the untutored question of the young which shatters the adult conception. The school removes children from everydayness, so that, when adults ride by in the new clothes of the emperor, they are not embarrassed by the children who might see their nakedness if they were not in school. The school, by being a separate place, separates the young from the publicness of interpretation, work, and political activity. In a sense, the rights of the child to participate in public life, to be free and to face the consequences of being free, have been abridged or perhaps never realized. Although we justify this abridgment of the rights of the young by the talk of protecting them, we are perhaps more likely to do it because we want to take our adult world for granted and not have it brought into question by the young. As a consequence, the young seldom feel that they participate in a public world, that they have rights to criticize it, to articulate their intentions and memories in response to it, or to reform it.

The idea of political and work activity as a form of activity interrelating the new being, the past, and community calls attention to the closed nature of the school and the need for open structures of education. But open must not be seen as simply a destruction of the walls that separate the school from other segments of society, or one segment of the school from another. Rather, an open place of education must be interpreted as a place where adults seek to influence the young, where the young seek to influence the adults; a place where the past as present may be used, interpreted, rethought, and reworked; a place not of submitting to someone else's power and accepted ways but of negotiating for power in the maintaining and reforming of the public world. Open education points to the search for communities by groups of people on pilgrimage, working the land with their tools, building the structures that house them from the elements, caring for those who are pushed into their presence, reshaping their life together, and telling and retelling the stories of where they have been and where they seem to be going.

NOTES

1. Richard E. Palmer, *Hermeneutics* (Evanston, Illinois: Northwestern University Press, 1969).

2. Paul Ricoeur, *Freud and Philosophy* (New Haven, Connecticut: Yale University Press, 1970).

3. Jurgen Habermas, *Knowledge and Human Interests* (Boston: Beacon Press, 1971).

IV. THE POLITICS OF CURRICULUM

Donald R. Bateman

I want to begin with some psychohistory, not deliberately for therapeutic purposes, but to try to provide a sense of where I have been and how that is related to where I am, for changes in any one consciousness reflect changes in the consciousness of others, and our collective sense of all this is the basis for dialogue.

Some of you may still remember the big curriculum development period, the days of Jerome Bruner, when "structure" and "discovery" led enterprising developers from academe into noble endeavors to save our children, and the schools that were destroying them, by creating new curriculum materials that were truthful, meaningful, learnable. Do you remember: Anyone can learn anything at any age if its structure is presented appropriately? We said that we must be innovative, that we must change. We sanctified those terms. We created curriculum development centers, research and development laboratories, college departments of educational change and development, and some of these ancient agencies still exist. We called together the experts to create teacher-proof materials, the assumption being, of course, that, if the right people produced highly structured programs, then even teachers would be unable to confuse things. We worked out elaborate plans for reorganizing space and time so we could use the teacher-proof materials in large groups, small groups, or with individuals for long or short periods of time. We constructed new buildings, mostly in the outer areas of the city, to implement new spatiotemporal arrangements. And, finally, since we did not really believe that curriculum materials could ever be teacher-proof, we tried to eliminate teachers altogether by producing programmed materials and teaching machines; it was sometimes called "individualized instruction." We even created mind-controlling TV programs for preschool children that extended the baby-sitting service Paul Goodman said the elementary school provided.

These so-called innovations, it turned out, were not innovations at all; instead, they consisted of old material in a new cover. Eighteenth-century prescriptive grammar, for example, is pretty insidious stuff whether it appears in an old-fashioned school book or in a programmed text with 3,200 frames. Even the "New Grammars" that school boards pay hundreds of thousands of dollars for are either old grammars with a new look or new grammars that linguists have discarded because they do not work. Or, alternatively, Robert Frost's fine poem "Stopping by Woods on a Snowy Evening" becomes an empty and cold exercise when one tries to experience it through John Ciardi's programmed critique of the poem. Notice that, implicit in all of this so-called innovative activity, is the conviction, still strong, that school failure is caused by the curriculum, aided by teachers and principals, perhaps even school boards in some not fully understood way, but not by colleges or teacher-training institutions or professors or curriculum developers, all of whom were presumably busy repairing the damage.

For most of a decade we were faced with perusing mountains of new materials created by experts, funded by the federal government, disseminated through the textbook industry, purchased by school boards; we have seen the products of the new educational technology—the remedial reading hardware, the programmed materials, the mathematical grammars; we have even sent master teachers aloft to lecture to thousands of students from the heavens—all of which did little to halt our growing awareness of the destructive nature of the whole educational enterprise from kindergarten through graduate school.

Running parallel to the allopathic medicine of the great curriculum reformers were the "Romantic School Critics," as they came to be called, sensitive to the lives of children, certainly a humanistic advance, and skeptical of the curriculum. John Holt put it well in the introduction to *How Children Fail:*

Most children in school fail. For a great many, this failure is avowed and absolute. Close to forty percent of those who begin high school, drop out before they finish. For college, the figure is one in three. . . . Why do they fail? They fail because they are afraid, bored, and confused. They are afraid, above all else, of failing, of disappointing or displeasing the many anxious adults around them, whose limitless hopes and expectations for them hang over their heads like a cloud. They are bored because the things they are given and told to do in school are so trivial, so dull, and make such limited and narrow demands on the wide spectrum of their intelligence, capabilities, and talents. They are confused because most of the torrent of words that pours over them in school makes little or no sense. It often flatly contradicts other things they have been told, and hardly ever has any relation to what they really know—to the rough model of reality that they carry around in their minds.[1]

It was useful to shift attention from the structure of disciplines to the lives and minds of children, but professors and suburban teachers did not believe it, or did not want to believe it, since their students seemed to do well, or at least most of them did, and that was because they were bright and motivated. It was probably only those poor children, who could not, or would not do the work, the Blacks and Puerto Ricans and Chicanos, or white children with dirty handkerchiefs and long hair, those children who were lazy and unmotivated and probably not very bright, as Jensen and others told us, who talked incorrectly, and wrote terribly, and could not read at all. Furthermore, Jonathan Kozol's *Death at an Early Age,* Herbert Kohl's *36 Children,* James Herndon's *The Way It 'Spozed to Be,* and other autobiographical documents of this sort seemed to verify this comforting hypothesis, making it legitimate for a new round of federal support for liberal solutions to the problems of the ghetto. Since it was clear that the problem was really in the schools, then we should fix up the schools, as well as the children who inhabit them, and eliminate poverty at the same time. Meanwhile the schools that were succeeding could proceed with their assignment to provide the country with the leaders of tomorrow.

But Holt was persistent, and so were Paul Goodman, Charles Silberman, and a host of others. Silberman said the problem was mindlessness. Holt said it was answer-centeredness:

Practically everything we do in school tends to make children answer-centered. In the first place, right answers pay off. Schools are a kind of temple of worship for "right answers," and the way to get ahead is to lay plenty of them on the altar. In the second place, the chances are good that teachers themselves are answer-centered, certainly in mathematics, but by no means only there. What they do, they do because this is what the book says to do, or what they have always done. In the third place, even those teachers who are not themselves answer-centered will probably not see, as for many years I did not, the distinction between problem-centeredness and answer-centeredness, far less understand its importance. Thus their ways of teaching children, and, above all, the sheer volume of work they give them, will force the children into answer-directed strategies, if only because there isn't time for anything else.[2]

All of this seemed to indicate that many of our children were failing, at least they were not learning how to learn, whether they lived in the suburbs or the ghetto, and, if the failure was more subtle in the one place than the other, it was no less alarming. It seemed to many that we had created a prison in which students and teachers distrusted each other. Students had to find the right answers to succeed, but they were forbidden to think, question, or challenge.

Suddenly, or at least it seemed sudden, students began to rebel, and there was a cry for relevance. This was what the Romantic Critics had been saying all along, and it gave them strength, or at least it seemed to until Ivan Illich came around and said we should disestablish schools, whatever that meant, or deschool society, which was puzzling and probably impossible. But there was magic in Illich, for awhile at least, even if he did not mean it. Holt went to Cuernavaca. The trip, along with the memory of Kent State and Jackson State, of Vietnam and the invasion of Cambodia, of Watts and Hough, of napalm and My Lai, was shared by others—if not in Mexico, in conferences and seminars, in books and articles. It led finally to some new understandings. Holt's new sense of it all appeared in the *New Schools Exchange Newsletter,* in which he said that,

truly good education in a bad society is a contradiction in terms. In short, in a society that is absurd, unworkable, wasteful, destructive, secretive, coercive, monopolistic, and generally antihuman, we could never have good education, no matter what kind of schools the powers that be might permit, because it is not the educators of the schools but the whole society and the quality of life in it that really educate ... More and more it seems to me ... that it makes very little sense to talk about education *for* social change, as if education was or could be a kind of getting ready. The best and perhaps only education for social change is action to bring about that change.[3]

He did not say what that action should be; he did say he was not proposing that we must change society before we change the schools but that society is the school, and, since "men being above all else looking, asking, thinking, choosing and acting animals, what they need above all else is a society in which they are to the greatest possible degree free and encouraged to look, ask, think, choose, and act; making this society, then, is the chief social or political and educational task of our time."

So schooling has nothing to do with it, or so it seemed, and our attention shifted from the school to the larger society, and suddenly it became easier to comprehend Illich's contention that the

enormous investment of money into schooling by underdeveloped
countries would not eliminate poverty; neither would it change the
economic status of underdeveloped people in developed countries. If
that was not clear, it became clearer when Kwame Nkrumah explained what neocolonialism is and sketched out in impressive detail
the economic web of international finance, controlled as it is by just
a few families whose members are in controlling economic positions
in bank after bank and conglomerate after conglomerate. But not
everyone could trust a foreigner, especially an African, even if he had
studied at the Universities of Lincoln and Pennsylvania, but a reporter named Felix Greene was around, and he wrote a book called
The Enemy, saying, like Pogo, "I have found the enemy and he is
us." If Nkrumah was too technical and a little dull at times, Greene,
carefully reportorial and with an abundance of documentation, was
quite clear, and so was neocolonialism, in both its national and international forms. Samuel Yette in a book called *The Choice: The Issue
of Black Survival in America* saw the racial aspects of both forms of
neocolonialism, and said so bluntly, again with more documentation
than white America could easily tolerate: "When the decade of the
1970's began," he said, "The United States government was offi-
cially—but unconstitutionally—in the midst of two wars: (1) a war of
'attrition' (that is, genocide) against the colonized colored people of
Indochina, and (2) an expeditionary 'law and order' campaign (that
is, repression or selective genocide) against the colonized colored
people of the United States."[4] And if that seems unbelievable, the
mass of evidence in the book would establish, for even the most
skeptical, its probability, and in another book, *The Warfare State,* by
another reporter, Fred Cooke, we get a clear account of the economic necessity of war and preparing for war and how the Penta-
gon's public relations program works and how much it costs. But
that is getting to be old stuff now that we are learning, in an unexpected gratuity from Watergate, that there are funds to convince the
people of the necessity for mining harbors and bombing at Christmas
and for invading countries and feting the returning heroes, and presumably for other things, too.

Once we shift our attention from the schools to the society we
begin to see that the central and primary theme of our age is domination: domination of the poor by the rich, Blacks, browns, reds, and
yellows by whites, women by men, students by teachers. It is called

neocolonialism, imperialism, racism, classism, sexism, all different though alike, related and interrelated in obvious and subtle ways. Those who dominate must develop ways of maintaining power, and they do this through institutions, one of which is schools. When a society is oppressive, as this one is, then the dominant pedagogy will be one developed by those in power; it will be domesticating, and, as Paulo Freire says in *Pedagogy of the Oppressed,* "it attempts by mythicizing reality, to conceal certain facts which explain the way men exist in the world; it resists dialogue; it inhibits creativity and domesticates. . . , thus denying men their ontological and historical vocation of becoming more fully human."[5] In contrast to this, a truly liberating pedagogy, "sets itself the task of demythologizing; it regards dialogue as indispensable to the act of cognition which unveils reality; it makes students critical thinkers; it bases itself on creativity and stimulates true reflection and action upon reality, thereby responding to the vocation of men as beings who are authentic only when engaged in inquiry and creative transformation."[6] The oppressed, Freire says, must participate in the development of the pedagogy of their liberation through discovering that they are the hosts, the servants, the benefactors of the oppressor. And as long as the oppressed live "in the duality in which *to be* is *to be like* and *to be like* is *to be like the oppressor,*"[7] they cannot contribute to the pedagogy of their liberation. Only as they discover that they and their oppressors are manifestations of dehumanization can they critically participate in their own liberation. This notion, as it has appeared in different forms at different times in different consciousnesses, has led some people to say publicly that the society of the oppressor, and the schools that teach us to accept it, is unacceptable. Keneth Kinnamon, speaking of these matters in *The English Journal,* put it not unlike Holt, but more to the political point:

For most young ghetto Blacks, integrationism is passé, irrelevant to the needs of the black masses and ideologically repugnant. Hence, a most serious dilemma, for the traditional function of American public education has been to socialize the child, to preach patriotism, to minimize group differences, to serve as a melting pot. But Blacks now want the schools to inculcate Black group awareness and pride, to expose the shams of a racist society, to prepare for Black self-determination leading to some kind of separatism. Not only are Blacks convinced that white America will *not* fully assimilate Blacks into the central patterns of the national life, but Blacks do not *want* such assimilation, for they see

America as Babylon, as an avaricious, sanguinary, imperialistic, faggoty, sterile, hypocritical, racist hell. Why integrate hell?[8]

It's a good question. Why, indeed? If this decadent empire is in its death throes, as Kinnamon says, then, as curriculum makers, or former curriculum makers, or educators, or creators of pedagogies, what is our task—to preserve it, to fix it through liberal reform, or to transform it?

As Richard Shaull says in the introduction to *Pedagogy of the Oppressed:*

> There is no such thing as a *neutral* educational process. Education either functions as an instrument which is used to facilitate the integration of the younger generation into the logic of the present system and bring about conformity to it, or it becomes "the practice of freedom," the means by which men and women deal critically and creatively with reality and discover how to participate in the transformation of their world. The development of an educational methodology that facilitates this process will inevitably lead to tension and conflict within our society. But it could also contribute to the formation of a new man and mark the beginning of a new era in Western history.[9]

The pedagogy of domination mythologizes reality; the pedagogy of liberation demythologizes it. There is no way to be neutral, no way to be apolitical.

But how is this integration of the younger generation into the logic of the present system accomplished? How is the mythology maintained? How do we demythologize?

Schooling is not neutral politically; it takes place in an institution designed and operated by those in power, to serve those who will come into power, to teach each child to accept his preassigned place: male or female, white or black, rich or poor, employed or unemployed. In short, schools channel children into the labor market and, as this assignment is accomplished, each child learns to accept the consequences of his success or failure and his subsequent place in society; he learns that it is right for the sons of doctors to become doctors, the sons of managers to become managers, the sons and daughters of laborers to become laborers, and the sons and daughters of the unemployed to be unemployed. This distribution of humanity into the marketplace is accomplished through tracking: grade levels and grading to show where and why you stand where you do in respect to the standards established by the test makers, why you are in the upper, middle, or lower track and, thus, college-, labor-, or unemployment-bound. To guarantee that this path to one's predestined place in the economy takes place smoothly and is acceptable to all, each child must internalize the cultural values that account for the necessity of his assignment. It is the purpose of the curriculum to accomplish this latter task.

Schooling is not neutral politically; nor is the culture it serves or the products of that culture that are selected for the curriculum. Any writer of history, of fiction, of poetry, of the news, of textbooks, or curriculum theory and curriculum guides, if he is alive enough to write in the first place, knows about genocide, racism, sexism, the systematic starvation of entire populations, the exploitation of third-world countries, the horrors of Christmas holiday bombings, and the illegal continuation of war. To be aware of such occurrences, whether writer, teacher, professor, researcher, and not to mention them "becomes more and more clearly a political act, an act of censorship or cowardice... When a cultural product presents a foreign war as the heroic effort of a master race to ennoble mankind, it serves imperialists, who make foreign wars against other races for profit; when a cultural product presents people who have no money or power as innately stupid or depraved, and thus unworthy of money or power, it is in the interests of the ruling class and the power structure as it stands; when a cultural product presents women who do not want to be household slaves or universal mothers or sex objects as bitches or sexual failures, it is in the interests of male supremacy."[10]

And so the curriculum of the pedagogy of domination is political; subtly or blatantly, by commission or omission, it teaches racism, sexism, classism. Take, for example, this excerpt from *Exploring New England,* a reader for fourth graders, part of the *New Unified Social Studies Program.* Robert, a young reader and a *dramatis personnae* in the book, is learning about the bravery of United States Army Captain John Mason in an engagement with the Pequot Indians:

His little army attacked in the morning before it was light and took the Pequots by surprise. The soldiers broke down the stockade with their axes, rushed inside, and set fire to the wigwams. They killed nearly all the braves, squaws, and children, and burned their corn and other food. There were no Pequots left to make more trouble. When the other Indian tribes saw what good fighters the white men were, they kept the peace for many years.[11]

Robert, engrossed in his reading and impressed by the bravery of Captain John Mason and his little army, says thoughtfully, "I wish I were a man and had been there."

And so, in one paragraph, a lesson in racism and sexism, a rein-forcement, no doubt, of many previous lessons, with more to come. It is not surprising that when James S. Coleman asked a cross section of high school students what they wanted to be that 31.6 percent of the boys said they wanted to be jet pilots.[12] It is also not surprising that we enthusiastically welcomed home the B-52 pilots as heroes and have forgotten the war, which continues but which interests us less since only Asians are dying.

So curriculum can be blatantly political, as it is, apparently, in the *New Unified Social Studies Program,* but it can also be subtly so, as it often is in the literature program. For example, one could cite William Butler Yeats's poem about the Easter Rebellion in Ireland in 1916, a poem that is read frequently in school. What was a matter of life and death to thousands of peasants and workers is reduced in the poem to an aesthetic moment in which Yeats says, "A terrible beau-ty is born." It doesn't matter who wins or who loses, whether the political ideas are right or wrong, but "whether individual heroism and aesthetic beauty are the products of their struggle." How differ-ent this poem is, that leads us away from the harsh verities of revolu-tionary struggle as perceived by a member of the aristocracy, from Bertolt Brecht's poem, "To Posterity," which is never read in school. Brecht, after hitting hard at the details of the personal sacrifice of revolutionary combat, ends his poem "by looking ahead with absolute confidence to a time after the revolution, when people will have changed, when circumstances will have ceased to require that they be as hard and purposeful as they needed to be. This is what is important to him, that the quality of life will change, and that peo-ple will cease to have to be deformed by their environment as he was."[13]

In similar ways, under the guise of reform, large, government-sponsored projects are politically motivated. Masters of grantsman-ship, responding to acknowledged social or educational inequalities, design extensive programs based on the pedagogy of domination. These consequently fail, for they neither touch the problem nor contribute to its solution. It is suddenly discovered, usually through pressure from the oppressed, that inner-city schools are in ghettoes, that inner-city schools are inhabited largely by black children, that black children are failing. The connections are made quickly: to succeed in school is to succeed in society; so, find a way to eliminate school failure and you eliminate the ghetto; so why do these children fail? They are deficient—not genetically, that would be a racist thing to say, Jensen notwithstanding, but environmentally. So, we have compensatory education—Upward Bound, a promising title, for the older children; Head Start, for preschool children. For the Upward Bound program the goal was "to turn these youngsters around . . . finding a way to boost the deflated self-esteem of the impoverished youngster. Convincing him of his own personal worth and ability to succeed *despite the deprivation of his background* is the key that releases the student to develop his potential."[14]

There were plans for the preschooler, too, and if it was too late for the Upward Bound students, as the explanation for the failure of the program claimed, we could expect the children in Head Start to be successful. Deprived children, we learned, need new experiences, and they come in two types: "(1) good and consistent examples of politeness, middle-class articulation, vocabulary, and neatness; and (2) a planned program to introduce the children through games, drills, etc. to various habits, manners, skills, and language arts already familiar to the middle-class child entering kindergarten. They will play house and, as they do, learn how to set the table, say 'please pass the butter,' answer the door or phone politely, etc."[15] This procedure is well known to Paulo Freire; it is called "cultural invasion," and it occurs when "the invaders penetrate the cultural context of another group, in disrespect of the latter's potentialities; they impose their own view of the world upon those they invade and inhibit the creativity of the invaded by curbing their expression."[16]

What was wrong with Head Start was that it didn't work. That suggested something to Bettye M. Caldwell, who said, in the *American Journal of Orthopsychiatry,*

the research literature of the last decade dealing with social-class differences has made it abundantly clear that all parents are not qualified to provide even the basic essentials of physical and psychological care to their children. . . There is, perhaps unfortunately, no literacy test for motherhood.[17]

So, step by step, back to the womb, or, just in case the genetic deficiency theory has some truth in it, perhaps copulation should be regulated, the participants screened, tested in reading and I.Q., and approved or disapproved according to the standard. And so, on to sterilization and genocide, the sure way to eliminate a racial problem. And if this sounds extravagant, let me remind you that in "April of 1970 President Nixon sent to the Department of Health, Education, and Welfare a recommendation from his personal physician that all children be tested at age 6 to identify criminal potential and that the potential criminals be 'treated' by being placed in state-run camps. And, in the same month, The Commissioner of Education, Dr. James Allen, proposed that all American children should be 'diagnosed' at age 2½ for 'home and family background, cultural and language deficiencies, health and nutrition needs, and general potential as an individual.' This information would then be computerized and sent to a 'team of trained professionals,' whose job it would be to write a detailed prescription for the child and, if necessary, for his home and family as well."[18]

I am happy to report, in regard to these matters, that in Ohio we are right on top of this problem, with two sterilization bills before the legislature, one for women on welfare who have two illegitimate children and one for men who cannot support their families. As the sponsor of the bills said, "If they live like animals, then they should be treated like animals."

The pedagogy of domination is strong; it seems ubiquitous at times, penetrating our institutions from the White House to the local school. Racism, sexism, classism—those deeply internalized social values—are at the root of our problems. They are deep in our psyches, and they cause our liberal reforms to fail because they treat the symptoms and not the causes. Even humanistic education, which has always seemed so attractive, from the early writings of Holt to the later ones of Maslow, tacitly accepts the class system with its racism, its gross commercialism, its male chauvinism, its institutional violence, its imperialistic wars—accepts them by failing to mention them, by pretending to be apolitical. It is a move in the right direction to reject the model of science, as Maslow does, because it is "positivistic, behavioristic, objectivistic, derived from the study of objects and things, value-free, value-neutral, and thus illegitimately used for the study of human beings." It is a "terrible technique," he says, that "has not worked."[19] The answer to Maslow seems to be humanistic education, not just aesthetic education. Something more than this is needed, but it must be self-actualizing. As a consequence, "We would have a great flowering of a new kind of civilization. People would be stronger, healthier, and would take their own lives into their hands to a greater extent. With increased personal responsibility for one's personal life, and with a rational set of values to guide one's choosing, people would begin to actively change the society in which they lived. The movement toward psychological health is also the movement toward spiritual peace and social harmony."[20]

It is attractive—the bringing together of the affective and the cognitive, the attainment of higher values, self-actualization, becoming more fully human. But there is a catch, and it runs through the romantic prescriptions for the new education. Maslow should know it well, but, if he sees it, he does not say so. What he does say is that "a child cannot reach self-actualization until his needs for security, belongingness, dignity, love, respect, and esteem are all satisfied."[21] Thus, humanistic education is for those who belong, for the secure, the dignified, the loved, the respected, and the esteemed, whoever they are; it is certainly not suitable for the oppressed, or perhaps it should be stated the other way around: the oppressed are not suited to it.

Christopher Jencks has recently said that "the primary basis for evaluating a school should be whether the students and teachers find it a satisfying place to be,"[22] which might lead us to say that humanistic school reform is necessary, but not sufficient; in fact, tinkering with the surface of things or treating the symptoms of deep underlying causes will not make much difference. Integration, decentralization, performance contracting, compensatory education, bidialectalism, experimental schools, sensitivity training, remedial reading, humanistic education—none of these liberal answers will contribute much to a pedagogy of liberation. The reformers, Jencks says, "are always getting trapped into claiming too much for what they propose. They may want a particular reform. . . because they think these reforms will make schools more satisfying places to work. Yet they feel obliged to claim that these reforms will also reduce the number of nonreaders, increase racial understanding, or strengthen family life. A wise reformer ought to be more modest, claiming only that a particular reform will not harm adult society and that it will make life pleasanter for parents, teachers, and students in the short run."[23]

What Jencks says is true, at least in regard to the effects of reform, but we should carefully note, since reform is part of the mythology of the pedagogy of domination, that a wise reformer should do no such thing, for if he did he would not only be contributing to the liberation of people by demythologizing the role of reform, he would be out of work, and so would a lot of other people.

The channeling of children into the labor market, and the concomitant domestication that justifies it, is as much a part of America as mom and apple pie, but the myths weaken a little as the demythologizing proceeds from Watergate to the analysis of the sexist and racist content of curricula, and though our schools and colleges, our reformers and leaders, our journalists and curriculum developers seem committed to the preservation of the status quo, knowledge is available; it is our task, each one of us, to come to grips with what is known, to take a stand, to decide whether to be a part of the problem or a part of the solution.

NOTES

1. John Holt, *How Children Fail* (New York: Dell Publishing Co., 1964), p. xiii.

2. *Ibid.*, p. 90.

3. John Holt, *New Schools Exchange Newsletter* No. 60, p. 20.

4. Samuel Yette, *The Choice: The Issue of Black Survival in America* (New York: Berkley Publishing Co., 1971), p. 11.

5. Paulo Freire, *Pedagogy of the Oppressed* (New York: Herder and Herder, 1970), p. 71.

6. *Ibid.*

7. *Ibid.*, p. 33.

8. Keneth Kinnamon, "Afro-American Literature, the Black Revolution, and Ghetto High Schools," *English Journal* 59 (No. 2, February 1970).

9. Freire, *Pedagogy of the Oppressed*, p. 15.

10. Meredith Tax, "Culture Is Not Neutral, Whom Does It Serve?" in Lee Baxandall (ed.), *Radical Perspectives in the Arts* (New York: Penguin Books, Inc., 1972), pp. 15-16.

11. Harold B. Clifford, *Exploring New England*, New Unified Social Studies (Chicago: Follett Publishing Company, 1961); cited in Paul Lauter and Florence. Howe, *The Conspiracy of the Young* (New York: World Publishing Co., 1970), p. 231.

12. J. S. Coleman, "Social Climates in High School," *Cooperative Research Monograph, 4* (Washington, D. C.: Office of Education, U.S. Department of Health, Education, and Welfare, 1961), p. 11; cited in Lauter and Howe, *Conspiracy of the Young*, p. 206.

13. See Meredith Tax, "Culture Is Not Neutral," pp. 18ff.; and Ellen Cantarow, "Why Teach Literature?" in Louis Kampf and Paul Lauter (eds.), *The Politics of Literature: Dissenting Essays on the Teaching of English* (New York: Pantheon Books, 1972), pp. 76-80.

14. "Upward Bound: War on Talent Waste at Indiana State University," a special issue of *The Teachers College Journal* 38 (January 1967); quoted in Lauter and Howe, *Conspiracy of the Young*, p. 268.

15. "Head Start or Dead End?" in Jeremy Larner and Irving Howe (eds.), *Poverty: Views from the Left* (New York: Apollo Editions, Inc., 1968), pp. 133-34; quoted in Lauter and Howe, *Conspiracy of the Young*, p. 273.

16. Freire, *Pedagogy of the Oppressed*, p. 150.

17. "What Is the Optimal Learning Environment for the Young Child?" *American Journal of Orthopsychiatry* 37 (1967), pp. 16, 17; quoted in Lauter and Howe, *Conspiracy of the Young*, p. 274.

18. Lauter and Howe, *Conspiracy of the Young*, p. 168.

19. A. H. Maslow, *The Farther Reaches of Human Nature* (New York: Viking Press, 1971), p. 170.

20. *Ibid.*, p. 195.

21. *Ibid.*, p. 190.

22. Mary Jo Bane and Christopher Jencks, "The Schools and Equal Opportunity," *Saturday Review* 55 (No. 38, September 1972), 41.

23. *Ibid.*, 42.

SELECTED REFERENCES

Baxandall, Lee (ed.). *Radical Perspectives in the Arts*, Pelican Book A 1423 (Baltimore: Penguin Books, Inc., 1972).

Berg, Ivar. *Education and Jobs: The Great Training Robbery* (New York: Praeger, 1970).

Cook, Fred. *The Warfare State*, Collier Books (New York: Macmillan, 1962).

Greene, Felix. *The Enemy*, Vintage (New York: Random House, 1970).

Holt, John. *How Children Fail* (New York: Dell Publishing Co., 1964).

Illich, Ivan. *Deschooling Society* (New York: Harper & Row, 1970, 1971).

Jencks, Christopher, *et al. Inequality: A Reassessment of the Effect of Family and Schooling in America* (New York: Basic Books, Inc., 1972).

Kampf, Louis, and Paul Lauter (eds.). *The Politics of Literature: Dissenting Essays on the Teaching of English* (New York: Pantheon Books, 1970, 1972).

Katz, Michael. *School Reform: Past and Present* (Boston: Little, Brown, 1971).

Kinnamon, Keneth. "Afro-American Literature, The Black Revolution, and Ghetto High Schools," *English Journal* 59 (No. 2, February 1970).

Larner, Jeremy, and Irving Howe (eds.). *Poverty: Views from the Left* (New York: Apollo Editions, Inc., 1968).

Lauter, Paul, and Florence Howe. *The Conspiracy of the Young* (New York: World Publishing Co., 1970).

Maslow, Abraham. *The Farther Reaches of Human Nature* (New York: Viking, 1971).
Nkrumah, Kwame. *Neo-Colonialism: The Last Stage of Imperialism* (New York: International Publishers Co., Inc., 1966).
Pateman, Trevor (ed.). *Counter Course: A Handbook for Course Criticism,* Penguin Educational Special (Baltimore: Penguin Books, Inc., 1972).
Rothstein, Richard. "Down the Up Staircase: Tracking in Schools," *This Magazine Is about Schools* 5 (No. 3, Summer 1971).
White, George Abbott, and Charles Newman (eds.). *Literature in Revolution* (New York: Holt, Rinehart, and Winston, 1972).
Yette, Samuel. *The Choice: The Issue of Black Survival in America* (New York: Berkley Publishing Co., 1971).

V. COGNITION, CONSCIOUSNESS, AND CURRICULUM

Maxine Greene

My theme derives in part from Paulo Freire, particularly from his notion that "liberating education consists in acts of cognition."[1] His context, of course, was a literacy program for Brazilian peasants, a learning situation in which persons were to be liberated through "action and reflection" on the world as they experienced it. They were to be enabled to identify the causes of their own oppressive reality, and, having understood those causes, they were to choose themselves as persons who could change the given into what they thought *ought* to be. Seeking implications for a theory of curriculum, I am not suggesting (nor do I think anyone ought to suggest) that North American students are oppressed in the way peasant populations are oppressed. There are distinctions to be made between the culture of silence imposed on South American Indians and the injustices characteristic of our own society—or the peculiar powerlessness experienced by the young people in our schools. Nevertheless, I find Freire's phenomenological approach to education suggesting new vantage points when I ask myself whether anything can be done in schools and what curriculum ought to signify in a world so dominated by bureaucracies and inhuman technological controls, when I consider the inequities and corruptions surrounding us today, and when I ponder ways of arousing students to choose themselves as persons who are committed, responsible, involved. Curriculum, I think, must be conceived in terms of possibility for individuals, all kinds of individuals. It must offer varying perspectives through which all kinds of people can view their own lived worlds. It must provide opportunities for them to see that they themselves, whoever they are, constitute those worlds as self-determining human beings existing with others in intersubjective community.

The social reality in which we have to try to create such a curriculum is increasingly structured by the schemata of those who think in terms of behavioral objectives, achievement testing, and management capability, and I think this has to be made clear. Talk of behavioral modification and engineering has become part of the educational given for many of our colleagues by now. B. F. Skinner is already celebrating the way in which environmental contingencies are taking over functions once attributed to autonomous man. When he describes his technology of behavior, however, he reassures us that his approach does not abolish man. "It is," he says significantly, "autonomous inner man who is abolished, and that is a step forward."[2] When looked at from a distance, many young people appear to accede. From the behaviorist point of view, they might even be said to be responding to positive reinforcements as they take up traditional life-styles, define economic goals for themselves, pursue what they think of as status and success. From the point of view of observers like William Pinar (who "see" quite differently from the behaviorists) a heightened consciousness is being achieved by increasing numbers. Peter Berger and his associates describe an ongoing "demodernization"[3] of youthful consciousness that makes questionable the claims of those who observe (and measure) from without. Demodernization entails a rejection of the engineering mentality, of efficiency and compartmentalization, of predefined life-goals. It may signify a growing perception by young people that these things compose an alien reality, in fact a mode of oppression. I think few of us would disagree that there are multiple signs of a persisting malaise, even among those remaining in our institutions. There is a sense of powerlessness expressed in cynicism and privatism, a loss of trust tinged with despair.

As I view it, our obligation as educators is to enable students to take action against such powerlessness, to take action to transcend what they now vaguely refuse. Our obligation is to enable them to perceive themselves as "subjects" rather than passive objects of control. Recognizing that, on some level, all behavior may be said to be caused, recognizing the degree to which individuals are manipulated, we need to confront the fact that learning is, as Michael Oakeshott puts it, "an activity possible only to an intelligence capable of choice and self-direction in relation to his own impulses and to the world around him."[4] Learning is significant only when it responds to personal necessity, to the learner's recognition that he personally is "condemned to meaning"[5] and must take responsibility for his own life. If it is indeed the case that the world is, in effect, meaning*less* for those who do not impose orders of their own, it is trivial to focus primarily on affect and sensitivity when attempting to help a learner resist false consciousness and control. Cognitive action is required: a naming of the world, a striving toward awareness of the self in action, of the forces that work to condition and those with the potential of setting the individual free. The learner must be enabled to take diverse vantage points on his own reality so as to understand in his own terms limitations and possibilities. And his learning must involve, as Merleau-Ponty puts it, a rediscovery "of my actual presence to myself, the fact of my consciousness which is in the last resort what the word and the concept of consciousness mean."[6]

We are all aware that consciousness does not mean mere innerness or introspection. When we think phenomenologically, we realize that consciousness means a thrusting toward the things of the world. It refers, in fact, to the multiple ways in which the individual comes in touch with objects, events, and other human beings. These ways of coming in touch include all the activities by means of which realities present themselves: perceiving, judging, believing, remembering, imagining.[7] We realize, too, that consciousness is characterized by intentionality. It is always *of* something—something which, when grasped, relates to the act of consciousness involved as the meaning of that act.

To illustrate, it is useful to turn to literature. I think of Herman Melville's story, "Bartleby the Scrivener," which deals with a nineteenth-century law office on Wall Street and what happens within the consciousness of the lawyer-narrator when a passive young man says repeatedly, "I prefer not to," while everyone else is simply doing what he has to do. When Bartleby, asked to compare a document he is copying with others, first says, "I would prefer not to," the lawyer gets angry, then sees the scrivener as an unearthly creature who has inexplicably wandered into his life. He thinks "there was something about Bartleby that not only strangely disarmed me but in a wonderful manner touched and disconcerted me." He is becoming aware of Bartleby's forlornness, and that forlornness may be described as the meaning of the particular act of consciousness expressed in what the lawyer says to himself. In a moment, however, the lawyer begins to reason, and Bartleby then means a threat to "common usage and common sense." Somewhat later, he regards the scrivener charitably, and Bartleby means, at that point, a way of purchasing "a delicious self-approval." And so it goes, as the lawyer moves from categorizing to judging to identifying. "The scrivener's pale form" presents itself to him in different guises throughout the story—and finally stands before the lawyer's mind in such a fashion that he alters the lawyer's life. "Ah, Bartleby!" he says to himself at the end, "Ah, humanity!" There are many other literary examples. I think of E. M. Forster's *Passage to India* and the way in which, through Mrs. Moore's fatigued acts of consciousness (her remembering, imagining, wondering) the echo of the Malabar cave presents itself: "Pathos, piety, courage—they exist, but are identical, and so is filth. Everything exists, nothing has value." Some will recall that this revelation probably accounts for Mrs. Moore's consequent death. I think of Kafka's K. being arrested at the start of *The Trial* and the way in which the two strangers present themselves to his mind: "Who could these men be? What were they talking about? What authority did they represent?" And I think of the acts of consciousness that follow—and of K.'s guilt, and of his death. Each of these characters—the lawyer, Mrs. Moore, K.—is speaking out of his or her life-world, his or her experienced context. Each of the fictions mentioned dramatizes the multiplicity of the acts of consciousness required for a disclosure of what is happening. The suspense in each story derives from the shocks the character involved experiences as he or she moves from one subuniverse of meaning to another and, most particularly, when he or she is forced to break with what has been taken for granted, with "socially constructed reality"[8]—a universe of prudence and entitlements for the lawyer; the constructs of British colonialism for Mrs. Moore; the ordinary existence of a well-meaning little clerk for K.

We can see in imaginative literature the perspectival nature of perception, something we overlook in daily life, and we are given opportunities to understand the differences between phenomenal or inner time and the time of the public world. These differences account in part for the discrepancy between the multiple acts of perception required for the disclosure of an object and the identity of the object-as-perceived. When I stand at a podium and look at a face in the audience, I am likely to regard that face as somehow given, identical from one moment to the other, objectively there. Actually, my perceiving of that face takes place within my inner time; there are multiple perceptions occurring, each one in some manner distinctive. Each one takes place at a different moment of my speaking, at a different stage in my life history. For all that, I see the face as identical. I am not aware of what Michael Polanyi calls my "subsidiary awarenesses."[9] I take a conventional or a "natural" attitude; I forget that I constitute my world.

If there is to be an explicit disclosure of that face, or of a golden bowl or a white whale, there must be some awareness of the multiplicity of perceptions, the shifting vantage points, the differing perspectives in relation to which the identity of the face—or the bowl, or the whale—is ascertained. The same is true of the desk on which I wrote this paper, the desk which appears to exist independently in an objectively real world. It is true as well of the public school system, the Watergate affair, the Civil War. None of these can be disclosed to the individual explicitly or fully if he is not aware of the events in his inner time that constitute them for him. Nor can he become fully rational until he becomes conscious of the way in which, in every case, "perspectives blend, perceptions confirm each other, a meaning emerges."[10]

It seems to me that personally significant and liberating learning can only take place when the learner is able to articulate and make explicit what is involved as "meaning emerges." Significant learning can only take place when the individual consciously looks from a variety of vantage points upon his own lived world, and when he achieves what Alfred Schutz calls a "reciprocity of perspectives"[11] upon his own reality. When he recognizes that he himself has blended those perspectives and permitted his perceptions to confirm one another, he knows that he himself has constituted meanings and brought whatever order there is into his own world.

I want to suggest that curriculum be conceived as a source of such perspectives rather than the carrier of some alien reality. I want to suggest that history, physics, literary criticism, and the rest be treated as subuniverses, as meaning to be achieved through free and informed engagement with their structures and in regard for their methodological norms. My hope is that students can be made aware of their role in constituting meanings, in making their own existence articulate. If they become so aware, they may come to the point of choosing themselves as questioners, perhaps as inquirers, for the sake of increasingly explicit disclosures of their worlds.

This, of course, can never happen if knowledge is treated as a secret horde or private property or what Dewey called "an immobile solid."[12] Nor can it happen if what Freire calls the "banking" approach is maintained, or if teachers talk about "reality as if it were motionless, static, compartmentalized, and predictable."[13] Nor can it happen if conventions of success and achievement are used to control individual learning, if fixed time schemes make it impossible to create patterns of meaning in inner time. And it will not happen if learners are not challenged to move out from their own subjectivities for the sake of taking diverse perspectives on their lives—the perspectives the sciences make possible, and the arts, person-to-person interchange, reverie, work, and play. Indeed, they ought to be provided opportunities for moving back and forth in self-chosen rhythm between what Arnold Stenzel describes as "landscape" (or prereflective consciousness)[14] and "geography" (the ordered materials of the disciplines), "the common world in which private landscapes become ordered and intersubjectively available."[15]

The trouble is, of course, that most people are too immersed in daily life to be aware of how they constitute their worlds. Taking for granted the commonsense appearances of things, governing themselves by the recipes others impose on them for structuring the intersubjective world, they function habitually and compliantly. They seldom, if ever, ask themselves what they have done—what they are doing—with their own lives, whether or not they have acted on their freedom or have acceded to the imposition of patterned behavior, the assignment of roles. It seems evident that the schools encourage immersion, deliberately or unthinkingly. The schools create the kind of reality that absorbs those within it and thereby serves to submerge consciousness. This, fundamentally, is the nature of the oppression they impose. This is what makes it so difficult for people to learn how to learn.

People continue in such submergence unless, as Albert Camus put it, "one day the 'why' arises and everything begins in that weariness tinged with amazement." The weariness comes "at the end of the acts of a mechanical life, but at the same time it inaugurates the impulse of consciousness."[16] The "why" may take the form of anxiety—the strange, nagging anxiety that occurs when a person realizes he is not acting on his freedom, not realizing possibility. Or it may accompany an outraged perception of the lacks or insufficiencies in ordinary life. It may arise in a sudden understanding of oppression and control. It may come with a feeling of disquietude when the reality of the laboratory gives way to the reality of the poetry class, when the classroom gives way to the workplace, the film to the ordinariness of the street. Or the "why" may arise in response to problem posing, to the kind of questioning aroused by a sense of impasse, the kind of questioning that may jolt individuals out of their immersion and make them reach toward the fringes of what they think they know.

I happen to believe that this kind of awakening can still occur in schools, at least where there are teachers who no longer lead mechanical lives. Having themselves experienced what it means to be aroused to weariness and amazement, they have to think of ways of awakening others, the others who are submerged. How can they be awakened to pursue the clarity needed for self-consciousness? How can they be persuaded to be vigilant, not only with respect to oppression, but with respect to abstraction and indifference—the indifference Camus (in another work) associated with "plague"? I believe that being in the world *in person* and caring about what happens (in Washington, in Phnom Penh, and down the street from the school yard) because all this is included in one's social reality have much to do with learning and making sense, with wanting to constitute meaning in the world. In *The Plague,* Tarrou and Dr. Rieux are both concerned with understanding and with naming, as they are with decency and with love. One evening they take "an hour off—for friendship" from their voluntary struggle against the pestilence, and Tarrou tells the story of his life. He has discovered, through his various experiences, that no one on earth is free from plague.

And I know, too, that we must keep endless watch on ourselves lest in a careless moment we breathe in somebody's face and fasten the infection on him. What's natural is the microbe. All the rest—health, integrity, purity (if you like)—is a product of the human will, of a vigilance that must never falter. The good man, the man who infects hardly anyone, is the man who has the fewest lapses of attention. And it needs tremendous willpower, a never ending tension of the mind to avoid such lapses. Yes, Rieux, it's a wearying business being plague-stricken. But it's still more wearying to refuse to be it.[17]

To have plague is not only to be indifferent; it is to be abstract, to use "big" words like humanization, democratization, and self-actualization in order to obscure what is actually happening between the person and his world. I want to stress the fact that Tarrou can only say all this after he has told the story of his life to someone, after he has recalled some of his earliest perceptions of the world and his gradual constitution of the meanings of "plague." At that moment of friendship, Tarrou may be regarded as someone moved to the asking of critical questions by his awakening to himself and his own reality. It is because he has been self-reflective, because he has attempted to recover his own past, his own biography, that he can conclude by saying that "our troubles spring from our failure to use plain, clean-cut language" and that he has resolved always to "speak—and to act—quite clearly, as this was the only way of setting myself on the right track." And when Rieux asks him if he knows what path to follow for attaining peace, Tarrou replies, "The path of sympathy."

I speak of all this because the recovery of one's own biography is necessary if one is to become aware of how one has constituted meanings in the course of one's life, how one has brought into being the traditions by which one lives and the horizons toward which one occasionally yearns. The learner, after all, is the one who must effect relationships among his manifold experiences. Merleau-Ponty points out that we witness at every moment "the miracle of related experiences, and yet nobody knows better than we do how this miracle is worked, for we are ourselves this network of relationships."[18] In order to know this, however, each learner must explore his own background consciousness. He must make his own deliberate effort to achieve the kinds of articulations within his mental life which compose his "historico-autobiographical existence"[19] as a human being within the world. If he does not, he will be unable to perceive the possibilities in the subject matter made available to him. The self-consciousness deriving from self-recovery may at least enable him to feel himself "to be a subject" and thereby able to escape, on his own initiative, from molds, labels, and controls.

The immersion promoted by the schools tends to obliterate the primordial, the perceptual background against which a person's first precarious perspectives are gained, and this makes it peculiarly difficult for that person to break with the given later on, as it makes it difficult for him to identify the themes in his biography that are truly significant—the kind likely to generate cognitive quests. Freire talks of such themes in connection with human aspirations, motives, and objectives, which are as historical as men themselves. "But—

precisely because it is not possible to understand these themes apart from men—it is necessary that the men concerned understand them as well. Thematic investigation thus becomes a common striving toward awareness of reality and toward self-awareness, which makes this investigation a starting point for the educational process or for cultural action of a liberating character."[20]

Looking toward curriculum and toward existing schools, I cannot but have in mind the prevalent suspicion of the "myth of objective reality."[21] Linked to it are kindred suspicions that organized knowledge, like Jacques Ellul's "technique," exists in relation to the system and apart from men. Taking Freire's view, I believe it is possible for human beings—teachers and learners, acting in concert—to appropriate such knowledge, to perceive it in the light of aspirations and objectives "as historical as men themselves." All depends on how the effort to generate knowledge structures is linked to relevant themes by persons who have refused the mechanical life.

The striving toward awareness and the thinking in which it culminates cannot be merely random if it is to result in mastery and "cultural action of a liberating character." To understand, after all, is to appreciate whole networks of conceptual relations, along with the appropriate bases for truth and validity involved. We cannot forget how rigorous an undertaking it is to generate any conceptual structure; and, simply because it is rigorous, we cannot avoid the necessity of involving students in justifying the effort required. It is not enough in this kind of society to motivate by talking of intellectual growth alone or of education being "all one with growing." Nor is it enough to argue (as Philip Phenix does) that mastery of the disciplines will counter estrangement and alienation by revealing "the nature of things."[22] Nor will it be very helpful to speak, as R. S. Peters does, about "being civilized" and putting oneself in the way "of something conducive to valuable states of mind."[23] Far more compelling is Freire's notion of "man's vocation" and the struggle to recover a lost humanity. To recover a lost humanity is to come in touch with oneself as a living being involved in a struggle with other human beings and, at once, with the aspirations human beings hold in common. Somehow we have to discover how to present learning as integral to the struggle Freire describes, and curriculum as a resource for transforming what exists.

Reared in a Deweyan tradition, few of us need reminding of the utility of problem-posing education, particularly when compared with mere transferrals of information. Nor must we be reminded of the significance of cognitive action, the mode of action that involves knowing what one is doing and doing things in a way that effects connections within experience, with a full awareness of the suitability of certain means to certain ends. We can assume that this would result in what Dewey described as a "constant reorganizing or reconstructing of the knower's experience" or " a direct transformation of the quality of the experience."[24] Meanings would become richer and more perceptible, Dewey would have said; the knower, or the learner, would increase his capacity to direct the course of his life.

Freire takes us beyond this view in several ways. One relates to the focal conception of praxis. The other has to do with consciousness of backgrounds, with "inner time." Praxis is a particular kind of cognitive action. It involves problem posing and problem solving, but it crucially involves, as well, the transcending or surpassing of the existing social situation. "Liberation is a praxis," writes Freire, "the action and reflection of men upon their world in order to transform it."[25] I would stress *"their* world" and the sense of brotherly or sisterly vocation that orients one to the common demands. Jean-Paul Sartre, discussing praxis as purposeful human activity, relates it to each individual's "fundamental project" and says that it signifies a refusal of some given reality "in the name of a reality to be produced."[26] The reality he describes relates directly to consciousness, as it does for Freire: the ways in which the world presents itself in its many phases to a mind thrusting outward into the situations in which the knower lives.

The problem theory of thinking also links thought to action, but not quite in the same way. For Dewey, thinking begins when equilibrium is temporarily lost, when uncertainties arise, when there is a fork in the road. Deliberating, the individual effects connections among the interests active in the situation: the moral considerations; his own inclinations; the activities it is possible for him to take; the consequences he can anticipate. Only as he clarifies the experiences involved can he decide intelligently upon a mode of action that will settle the original difficulty. When he finally decides, he has in mind a state of affairs he wishes to bring into being, the quality of which depends in large measure on the quality of thought marking the course of his inquiry. But the main concern is to resolve the original doubt, to overcome the obstacle, to make forward movement possible again.

Learning, Dewey said, is "something the individual *does* when he studies. It is an active, personally conducted affair."[27] The difficulty is that the pragmatist tends to take social reality—or the social-cultural matrix—for granted as a given, like the fork in the road. Alfred Schutz says that "intersubjectivity, interaction, intercommunication, and language are simply presupposed."[28] Similarly presupposed is the persistence of what Dewey called "social control." Freire, in contrast, insists on a "plenitude of praxis" or a critical reflection that increasingly organizes thinking and leads men "to move from a purely naïve knowledge of reality to a higher level, one which enables them to perceive the *causes* of reality."[29]

It is clear enough that Dewey also hoped to guide development from a "naïve knowledge" to more inclusive understanding, but there is little evidence that he was concerned with reflection on the causes of reality or of social control. Freire's view, which I think can be made relevant to teaching within the schools, demands that individuals begin not only with the posing of relevant questions but also with a clear sense of "a reality to be produced." They cannot, he believes, break with naïve knowledge without some intention to carry out a preconceived project, "to bring about the projected state of affairs."[30]

There must be an unveiling and a gradual disclosure of inner and outer horizons if learners are to be enabled to conceive such projects and take action to carry them out. Working in a dialogical relation with students, the teacher must try to move himself and them to ask the kinds of worthwhile questions that lead to disclosure and engage individuals in praxis. These are the kinds of questions that enable learners to perceive their own realities from many vantage points. They are the kinds of questions that enable them to identify lacks in their life situations and to move toward repair and transcendence. It is out of such perceptions, I believe, that cognitive action arises. It is against the background of such questioning that individuals reach out to constitute meaning in their lives. Somehow, the struggle to master the cognitive structures composing curriculum must be made continuous with the quest for meaning to which both teachers and learners are condemned. Freire talks of the cognized object—the subject matter or the discipline—existing between the teacher and the learner, both of whom are engaged in investigations and pursuits of meaning. And he talks of risking acts of love in the process, of discovering the kind of solidarity that becomes possible only when those being taught are recognized by their teachers (or their coinvestigators) as persons with the potential for transforming the reality they share with others, for surpassing their common world.

For a theme to be relevant for an individual, it must always relate to interest situations that are relevant. If it does, it can then be transformed into a problem "to which a solution, practical, theoretical, or emotional, must be given."[31] The concern for themes and the interest in zones of relevance discoverable in each person's biography differentiate this approach once more from that of the pragmatist. Most significantly, I think, the awareness of the import of oppression differentiates it, especially the oppression that accompanies an "invasion" on the part of those Freire calls "well-intentioned professionals."[32]

Take, for example, a college teacher confronting students in a social science class. He may know enough to understand that they are disgusted with the marking system and the routine, and that some of them blame the bureaucracy of the institution for what seems to be wrong. Sensitive himself to the pressures of the system, the teacher may realize that it is not enough to proffer the students a gift of freedom by releasing them into their own subjectivities and allowing them simply to express themselves, to be. He may be more concerned with stimulating them to learn how to learn and, by so doing, to equip themselves for the kind of action likely to transform some aspect of the encroaching bureaucracy. For all their vague unease, the students are, more than likely, effectively domesticated. They may reject for many reasons the teacher's efforts to arouse them to inquiry. The teacher will almost certainly be tempted to dominate them in the name of wide-awakeness and their own salvation. Yet, he also hopes to create a situation in which they will freely reach out for their own new perspectives and try to discover the nature of their own worlds. He must, even in the face of his desire to inspire and thus to dominate, present himself, as someone who is with his students as a coinvestigator in the field of history or economics, each one presented as a possibility. Along with the class, he may settle on the problem of the existing socioeconomic system in his search for a relevant theme. In dialogue, teacher and learners together may isolate certain dimensions of the system as thematically relevant. It may be the grading system or required classes or the pervasive impersonality. It may be the matter of credentials, or licensing requirements, or job opportunities. Whatever it turns out to be, it may be well to locate it in some outer horizon for a while, to be examined after inner horizons are explored. If inner horizons are not explored, there will be little possibility of linking deeply felt human aspirations to the subject of the investigation. More seriously, there will be little possibility of discovering the causes of existing reality and the ways in which, in individual life histories, it came to be.

Various people's recollections may be evoked, recollections of initial encounters with authority figures, with labels, with feelings of worthlessness, with expectations. There may be a trading of memories, an interchange, until certain people begin to see that their knowledge of systems and authorities and credentials is a consequence of a sedimentation of meanings, a result of mental processes that have gone on throughout their lives. If they can penetrate the history of such meanings, they may be enabled to effect relationships within the field of their own consciousness, interpreting their own pasts as they bear upon the present, reflecting upon their own judging and knowing, on the ways in which the world has presented itself through the years of their lives. This reflexive consideration of the activities of consciousness, this synthesizing of materials in inner time may have the effect of freeing individuals. It may enable them to understand that they, living in an intersubjective community and acting within it, have constituted the meanings of their own experiences, the meanings by which they live. Aware that others, too, from their distinctive vantage points, are doing the same, aware of the impact of social formulas and conventional interpretations on all their lives, they may undergo a "weariness tinged with amazement." They may be ready for critical reflection, ready to see.

At this point, teacher and learners may confront the outer horizons, the larger social situation that gave rise to their first unease. Now questions can be posed with respect to school experiences, work experiences, dealings with bureaus and bureaucracies. And each one may be able to ask "Why?" in his own voice, the nature of the "Why?" being determined by what each one most deeply knows. How can they account for the giantism, the depersonalization in the institutions they have known? Why the pressure on them to conform? Why the uncritical approbation of technological advancement? Why the subjection to experts, to knowledge as commodity? Why the indifference to mechanized killing? Why the destruction of the wilderness? Why the work ethic? Why a credentialing system? In intensifying dialogue, the teacher may direct attention to the fringes of what they all appear to know, to horizons where things are still vague, being only approximately understood. They may be horizons, in fact, never visible before. And it may be possible only to disclose them by looking through unfamiliar perspectives, by generating particular disciplines.

I am suggesting that the person brought to self-awareness by means of dialogue, made conscious of his own consciousness and conscious of sharing the earth with others, is far more likely to feel a desire for orientation or a desire to constitute a range of meanings than the one who is confronted in isolation with independently existing knowledge structures. I am suggesting, too, that the student who is moved (in response to his amazed and deeply felt questions) to break through the everyday to the horizons is more likely than we suspect to choose a struggle for disciplinary mastery. I am suggesting, in fact, that disciplinary learning in response to worthwhile questions can be a means of rejecting domination, even within oppressive and dominating schools.

"Liberating education consists of acts of cognition." The one who can look from diverse vantage points, who knows that he must constitute his world, is the one who is free to think about producing a new reality in association with others. In the name of that new reality, he is likely to seek higher knowledge in the effort to organize his thinking and constitute with his brothers and sisters a richer, more unified, less unjust world.

Must we, in some new and rebellious orthodoxy, treat the "system" as a given, impervious to rejections and to change? Can we not, as persons committed to transcendence, engage ourselves with fellow learners to widen and diversify perspectives? Can we not stimulate within ourselves and those we come to love a fresh awareness of the questionable, of what must not be taken for granted any longer? Can we not begin beckoning insistently, challenging individuals to move beyond the domestic and oppressive, to surpass the everyday?

NOTES

1. Paulo Freire, *Pedagogy of the Oppressed* (New York: Herder and Herder, 1970), p. 67.

2. B. F. Skinner, *Beyond Freedom and Dignity* (New York: Alfred A. Knopf, 1971), p. 200.

3. Peter L. Berger, Brigitte Berger, and Hansfried Kellner, "Demodernizing Consciousness," *Social Policy* 3, No. 6 (March-April 1973), 3-10.

4. Michael Oakeshott, "Learning and Teaching," in R. S. Peters (ed.), *The Concept of Education* (New York: Humanities Press, 1967), pp. 156-57.

5. Maurice Merleau-Ponty, *Phenomenology of Perception* (London: Routledge Kegan Paul, Ltd., 1962), p. xix.

6. Merleau-Ponty, *Phenomenology*, p. xvii.

7. Aron Gurwitsch, *The Field of Consciousness* (Pittsburgh, Pennsylvania: Duquesne University Press, 1964), pp. 3-6, 268.

8. Peter L. Berger and Thomas Luckmann, *The Social Construction of Reality* (New York: Anchor Books, 1967), p. 189.

9. Michael Polanyi, "The Structure of Consciousness," in Marjorie Grene (ed.), *Knowing and Being* (Chicago: University of Chicago Press, 1969), p. 214.

10. Merleau-Ponty, *Phenomenology*, p. xix.

11. Alfred Schutz, *The Problem of Social Reality*, Collected Papers, I (The Hague: Martinus Nijhoff, 1967), pp. 167-68.

12. John Dewey, "The School and Society," in Martin S. Dworkin (ed.), *Dewey on Education*, (New York: Teachers College Bureau of Publications, 1959), p. 47.

13. Freire, *Pedagogy*, p. 113.

14. Quoted in Donald Vandenberg, *Being and Education* (Englewood Cliffs, New Jersey: Prentice-Hall, Inc., 1971), pp. 83-85.

15. *Ibid.*, p. 85.

16. Albert Camus, *The Myth of Sisyphus* (New York: Alfred A. Knopf, 1955), p. 13.

17. Albert Camus, *The Plague* (New York: Alfred A. Knopf, 1948), p. 229.

18. Merleau-Ponty, *Phenomenology*, p. xix.

19. Alfred Schutz, *Reflections on the Problem of Relevance*, ed. Richard Zaner (New Haven, Connecticut: Yale University Press, 1970), p. 132.

20. Freire, *Pedagogy*, p. 43.

21. See Theodore Roszak, *The Making of a Counter Culture* (Garden City, New York: Doubleday Anchor Books, 1969).

22. Philip H. Phenix, "The Disciplines as Curriculum Content," in Donald Vandenberg (ed.), *Theory of Knowledge and Problems of Education* (Urbana: University of Illinois Press, 1969), p. 196.

23. R. S. Peters, *Education as Initiation* (London: Evans Brothers, Ltd., 1963), p. 15.

24. John Dewey, *Democracy and Education* (New York: The Macmillan Company, 1916), p. 89.

25. Freire, *Pedagogy*, p. 66.

26. Jean-Paul Sartre, *Search for a Method* (New York: Alfred A. Knopf, 1963), p. 92.

27. Dewey, *Democracy and Education*, p. 390.

28. Schutz, *The Problem of Social Reality*, p. 53.

29. Freire, *Pedagogy*, p. 98.

30. Schutz, *The Problem of Social Reality*, p. 67.

31. Schutz, *Collected Papers* (The Hague: Martinus Nijhoff, 1967), III, 124.

32. Freire, *Pedagogy*, p. 389.

VI. A TRANSCENDENTAL DEVELOPMENTAL IDEOLOGY OF EDUCATION

James B. Macdonald

The title of this chapter was prompted by the recent Kohlberg and Mayer article entitled "Development as an Aim of Education."[1] They talk about three ideologies: romantic, developmental, and cultural transmission. It is clear to me that there are at least two other potential ideologies that I am calling radical and transcendental developmental. I shall attempt to step off from Kohlberg and Mayer's framework to discuss briefly the radical ideology and to develop what I believe to be a transcendental developmental ideology. It is my contention that the radical and transcendental ideologies are the most potentially useful in the modern world.

The elements or components of ideologies as described by Kohlberg and Mayer are psychological theories, epistemological components, and ethical value positions. These correspond roughly with the philosopher's concern for ontological, epistemological, and axiological considerations. Essentially this amounts to a statement of the nature of man, the nature of knowledge, and the nature of values.

The romantic ideology Kohlberg and Mayer perceive is fundamentally concerned with human nature and the unfolding or maturation of the individual. Knowledge in this ideology is said to be existential or phenomenological, and it refers directly to the inner experience of the self. Truth is self-knowledge and extends to others by sympathetic understanding of other selves. The ethical theory of the romantic is based upon the freedom of the individual to be himself, assuming that individuals, when free, are essentially good unless society makes them otherwise.

The cultural transmission ideology is grounded in behaviorist psychology. Essentially the individual is shaped by his environmental experiences in terms of the associations and stimulus-response sets he encounters and acquires. Knowledge is the outer reality, the "objective" world, that can be found in sense experience and culturally shared. Value theory is either an ethically neutral stance or a social relativism that accepts the present cultural values for which there would appear to be consensus.

Between these two, in the sense that it is neither a model of inner experience or outer experience but a dialectic between inner and outer, lies developmental ideology. The transaction itself creates reality which is neither an inner nor an outer phenomenon, but something else. Dewey's method of intelligence and the cognitive-developmental work of Piaget with its concern for inner structures and outer structures encountered in interaction are the psychological models for this ideology. Knowledge is equated with a resolved relationship between inner experience and outer reality. Truth is pragmatic in that it depends upon its relationship to the situation in which we find ourselves. Values are based upon ethical universals derived philosophically, and they serve as developmental means and ends. Thus rational ethical principles, not the actual values of the child or the culture, serve as arbiters for defining aims.

Analysis of these ideologies suggests that the following elements are the critical aspects of ideology. Figure VI-1 illustrates this:

Figure VI-1 is of course highly simplistic, but it illustrates the inner and outer aspects of ideology and the dominant directions of the critical flow of the human encounter. Thus, the romantic conception is mainly from inner to outer, the cultural transmission from outer to inner, and the developmental is dialectical.

Kohlberg and Mayer assume that the radical position is equivalent to the romantic, or at least they use these terms interchangeably at times. This I believe to be in error. It is in error, that is, if radical is meant to imply political radicalism of a Marxian persuasion.

The political radical is committed to a dialectical model, as is the developmental. However, as the work of Paulo Freire[2] shows, it has a fundamentally different interpretation of the dialectic.

The developmental and radical models look identical only on the surface, for the radical model is weighted on the side of social realities. The developmental model is weighted on the side of inner cognitive structures. The progressive position assumed that democracy was the ideal social reality and continued its analysis of the interaction process with that assumption in mind. The radical model, on the other hand, is essentially based upon an analysis of why democratic ideas are not realized, thus emphasizing environmental structures.

(A) Romantic

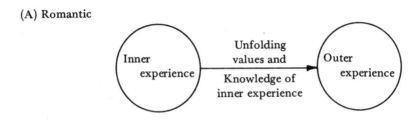

(B) Cultural transmission

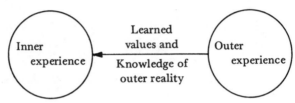

(C) Developmental

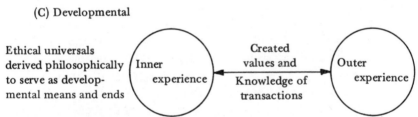

Figure VI-1. Elements in educational ideology

We still do not generally recognize this radical thrust in curriculum thinking, but the growing edge of writing in the past five or ten years leans toward a resurgence of romanticism and a renewal of past reconstructionist terms of the radical tradition. Neither is, I believe, the same as its predecessor, and I shall try to use historical perspective to validate both assertions.

The political view of curriculum that appears to provide the most satisfying analysis is Marxian in orientation. There are classical and Neo-Marxian differences of opinion that are of great interest and

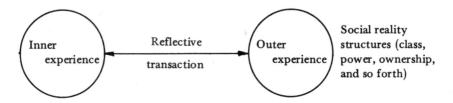

Figure VI-2. Model of praxis

impact. However, I shall try to generalize the radical position as an ideology in terms of what Kohlberg and Mayer left out.

The radical point of view takes off from the essential proposition that the critical element in human life is the way people live together. It further posits that the way people live together is determined essentially by the structure of our economic arrangements, the ownership of means of production, and the distribution of goods and services through the possession of power.

It is the social structures of the environment that provide the radical with his developmental impetus, rather than the biological structures of development in the individual that are so important for the liberal or progressive. This is not to say that either group ignores the other, but it is to say that the democratic ideal of the liberal as the social condition best able to foster individual development leaves much to be desired in terms of its usefulness for a historical analysis of why democracy appears to operate in a rather different manner than its rhetoric would suggest. Thus, the radical ideology raises questions that could lead us to another level of analysis of the curriculum.

At this level of analysis, radical ideology claims that liberal developmental ideology and romantic ideology are embedded in the present system. That is, the emphasis upon the individual and his unfolding or developing necessitates an acceptance of the social structures as status quo in order to identify in any empirical manner the development of the individual. Thus, developmental theory is culture and society bound, and it is bound to the kind of a system that structures human relationships in hierarchical dominance and submission patterns and alienates the person from his own activity in work and from other people. Given the level of analysis of the radical, the individual cannot fully develop out of the very conditions that are central to the improvement of human life. Only when new social conditions arise will we be able to begin to empirically identify and talk about human development in the new social context.

At this level of questions a radical curriculum thinker might ask:

1. How are the patterns of human relationships found in the broader society revealed in schools?
2. What function does the school have in the system, and how does this affect practices?
3. Why is there unequal opportunity to learn in schools, at least in terms of race and social class?
4. Why are textbooks biased in terms of race and sex, and why is history nonauthentic or biased?
5. Do schools provide for unequal access to knowledge by the way they operate?
6. How should we structure human relationships in school?

There are, of course, radical answers to such questions. However, questions tend to frame the answers we get, and the critical point here is that educational problems become quite different when one looks at them from a radical perspective.

My problem with the radical or political view of curriculum is not its level of analysis or the questions it asks, per se; instead, it is the feeling I have that it is also one step behind the world. Thus, I feel that, as McLuhan once said, we are traveling down a superhighway at faster and faster speeds looking out the rearview mirror. Kohlberg and Mayer's three ideologies are "over the hill," so to speak, but the political view is in the mirror. It does provide us with some idea of how straight the road is ahead provided our speed does not exceed our reaction time. What we need is some way to look beyond, if only a few feet.

The radical view of education in its political manifestations does provide us with a historical analysis—as well as with concepts for analyzing contemporary phenomena. Yet I find this historical view limiting in its materialistic focus, and I suspect that it is grounded fundamentally in the Industrial Revolution and reflects the same linear rationality and conceptualizing that characterizes the rise of science and technology. It is a "social science" of human relations and a "science" of history. Like all history, this is a special reading of the past that helped make sense out of the nineteenth-century present. The world today is not the same, and a different reading of history is needed to help make sense of our contemporary world.

The radical-political perspective as a base for curriculum thinking does not adequately allow for the tacit dimension of culture: it is a hierarchical historical view that has outlived its usefulness both in terms of the emerging structure of the environment and of the psyches of people today. I propose that the structure of the world environment today must be approached through the existence of a nuclear, electronic-computerized, multimedia technology rather than the more linear, single-media machine world. Further, I would propose that concomitant psychological structures in individuals must be viewed in a different perspective. I would like to reflect briefly upon these two ideas and then project some new questions for curriculum thinking.

Our present technology and our present world population have restricted our political options in ways we could not have readily foreseen. We are faced with such problems as energy crises that threaten the very survival of members of our population. Short of detechnologizing society, we are faced with the fact that political action that in any way threatens our fundamental technological cultural base is no longer a viable alternative unless we are willing, in the name of ideals, to inflict untold suffering and the threat of extinction on millions of human beings. Freedom to stop the workings of "the system" via revolution of some sort is no longer simply a threat to the power factions in our society; it is indeed a threat to all human beings.

I believe we have entered a new hierarchical level with our electronic world. This passage may have seemed gradual, but its impact has essentially been to produce a difference in kind (instead of in degree) in the condition of human existence. The institutionalization of nuclear and electronic technology, though dependent upon what its industrial predecessor has contributed, is an operating pattern, a cultural milieu that has never existed before.

The sense of powerlessness and impotence we feel is not a sign of alienation in the traditional Marxian sense. It is a true reflection of the state of the human beings to the extent that we transfer psychological states grounded in a premodern society. With an industrial psychological outlook we are indeed powerless when we consider our destructive nuclear capacity and our dependence upon computers and power sources to simply maintain our existence. No longer are we dominated by the owners of the tools of work; they are also dominated by the need for survival and power sources.

We have in effect created our first man-made gods in material form. We have created a human condition that, should it collapse by disaster or human direction, would destroy rich and poor alike. Now all people must serve the technical "gods" in some nonthreatening way in order to insure social and perhaps personal survival. Political action and political analysis of the human condition is now too limited a perspective with which to view our conditions of existence. They can threaten our very survival if used by people having an outmoded attitudinal structure. Precisely because radicals have been so busy pushing and tugging at the means of production and distribution, they do not see that they share the same technological world view—what liberals love, radicals hate, and both are equally possessed by technology.

A key phenomenon in understanding this transition is television. It is incomprehensible to me how people raised as children in a non-television world can miss the fact that the youth of today have been and are being dramatically affected by this overriding multimedia impact on their lives. To grow up with television is to grow up in an obviously mediated world.

Curriculum thinking should be grounded in cultural realities. One may see cultural realities in terms of a relativistic perspective or in long-range developmental terms. In my own developmental speculation I see the present and future technological domination of man as a step in the road toward human evolution. It is my personal myth that today's technology is yesterday's magic. Further, it is my intuitive feeling that technology is in effect an externalization of the hidden consciousness of human potential. Technology, in other words, is a necessary development for human beings in that it is the means of externalizing the potential that lies within. Humanity will eventually transcend technology by turning inward, the only viable alternative that allows a human being to continue to experience oneself in the world as a creative and vital element. Out of this will come the rediscovery of human potential.

SOCIAL SIGNALS OF TRANSCENDENCE

We are not completely without sociological validation of a transcendent ideology. Peter Berger,[3] for example, has presented a sociological analysis of human behavior that is relevant. Berger suggests that the one major implication of modern relativistic sociology is that it relativizes the relativizers as well. That is, taking a relativistic position also puts the relativists in the historical position of having their doctrine relativized.

He suggests that we examine the behavior of people and look empirically, using sociological methods, for what he calls signals of transcendence. In so doing, Berger finds as a beginning hypothesis that there are at least four such signals, that is, prototypical human gestures: the propensity for order and the automatic assurance of the adult to the child that everything is all right (that is, you can trust the world); the existence of play; the existence of hope; and the existence of damnation. Berger finds these gestures difficult to explain without some sense of transcendence. The propensity to order and have faith and trust in the meaning of things, playing, hoping, and the sense of indignation that some human actions lie beyond the acceptable are all unnecessary and inexplicable if everything is simply relative and realistic. Humor is also difficult to explain in such a context.

Thus, humans have both the propensity to play and laugh as if we need not be serious and the propensity to trust, order, and damn with a seriousness that transcends everyday political and economic concern. The case for nothing but social reality and psychological development, he feels, must be proved by the proponents of those views, not by those who see signals of transcendence.

The doors of human conception opened and ushered in the technological revolution. Political thinking is a rational social adjunct to a conceptual culture. Now we are facing the opening of the doors of perception in human experience, not as the minor mystical phenomena that have appeared throughout history, but as a large-scale movement of consciousness on the part of our young. A multimedia world is perceptual, not linear, in the utilization of concepts, but patterned concepts are received upon impact as perceptual experience. The psychological attitude born in this culture is a psychology of individuation, not individualism or socialism.

The human race is beginning to take another major step into the unknown source of its imagination, that same source that has created technology and all of the cultural trappings we possess. The signs are apparent in today's world and in the history of human *being.* In a very real sense it is as if we are coming to know that what we have imagined and conceptualized resides within us as potential, rather than having to be made into conceptual and material form.

Think for a moment about the mysteries of human experiences rather than our achievements. How can people walk on coals as hot as 2500 degrees without visible signs of burning on either their feet or clothing? What explains the various forms of extrasensory perception? How can people dream the future? What are teleportation, telekinesis, and similar experiences? What is a mystical experience?

You may write them off as empirically unfounded, just as Julius Caesar would have written off the technological world of today as utter impossibility. But the testimony of human history in terms of witnessing and personal experience cannot be ignored, for it is out of this very source of the unknown that whatever we have achieved has emerged. There is no reason to suspect that we have realized our human potential, and there is reasonable evidence that we may be rapidly approaching a new level of psychological and cultural growth from which dramatically new understandings of human potential will emerge.

It is my best guess that the next step, already begun, is an inward journey that will manifest itself by discovery, through perception and imagery, of human potential only slightly realized until now, and an outer journey for new communal life stages that are pluralistic and limited to small groups (tribes?) of people. The new communities will, of necessity, not threaten the technological superstructure that supports life, but they will seek pluralistic life styles within the superstructure.

A TRANSCENDENTAL DEVELOPMENTAL IDEOLOGY

A transcendental ideology seems to be necessary because I find the source of value positions to be inadequate in the other four. It is never clear on what basis or by what source the values of objective neutrality, social relativism, or ethical principle are derived. In other words, I find all four ideologies unclear in their ontological and phenomenological grounding.

There are two directions I could take at this point: the transcendental or the hermeneutic. I am not now equipped to pursue the latter course. From what I do know of this line of analysis, it seems to result in a cultural relativism that I find unacceptable at present. I will leave this door ajar for further study, however. What follows is fundamentally addressed to critical problems I see in the four ideologies described earlier.

My position is best approached through the concept of a dual dialectical process. A dialectic exists not only between the individual and his environment but also within the individual himself. Figure VI-3 will help to illustrate what I mean.

The relatively closed portions of Figure VI-3 represent the explicit knowledge systems of the individual and the situational context within which he acts. This represents a position similar to that held by radical ideologists, as far as it goes. Thus, I would agree that human activity is in part created by the reflective transaction of human consciousness in situational contexts.

It is clear, however, that, within the limits of the closed part, there can be no access to values or ethical principles that do not arise out of a utilitarian reflection upon the objective historical or personal consequences of human activity. Without positing a method of reflective intelligence based upon an analysis of the consequences of human activity, there could be no assessment of "good" other than a bare survival adjustment to reality, much in the manner of most other animals.

Utilitarianism as a source of values is, however, a relatively unsatisfactory position. It does not allow for or account for phenomena in human experience that have been readily apparent to persons throughout history and in contemporary society. Central to this discontent is the cognitive orientation of reflection as the method of intelligence and the only source of analysis for human activity. Thus, an a priori valuing of rationality is necessary in utilitarianism. Where does it come from?

That this gives only a partial account of human being is indicated by the second dialectic, between the explicit awareness of the individual and the nonexplicit nature of the individual. The self, in other words, is composed of both conscious awareness and unconscious data at any given time.

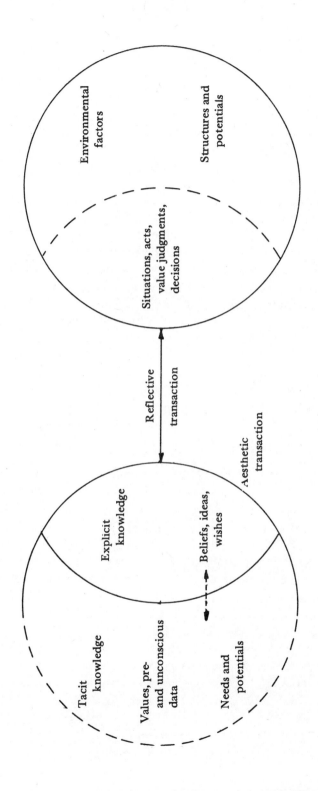

Figure VI-3. A dual dialectic

Values, I believe, are articulated in the lives of people by the dual dialectic of reflecting upon the consequence of an action and sounding the depths of our inner selves. Only a process something like this can explain why "what works is not always good." Some dual dialectic is also needed to explain the existence of reason, or aesthetic rationality, to counterbalance purely technological rationality.

The self as a concept has suffered at the hands of everyone from behaviorists to analytical philosophers. I find this interesting but neither the empirical reductionism of behaviorists nor the analysis of common usage convince me that there could not be an agency where phenomenological experience would permit the analyst to analyze and the behaviorist to behaviorize. Neither come to grips with what allows them to perform at all. I find the concept of self as an experiencing agency to be useful for this purpose, and I would suggest that a self is no less mystical than a culture or a society since all three can only be structured as hypothetical constructs by some languaging agency.

The inner dialectic of the self is a critical element if we are to advance the position that culture is in any way created by human being. The possibility of value may well be limited in alternatives by the individual-biological-social dialectic, but the validation of values would seem to demand some source other than explicit and rational knowledge.

Herbert Marcuse[4] seemed to recognize a need for something similar—a new sensibility as well as a raised level of critical consciousness —in the idea of aesthetic rationality. Aesthetic rationality, Marcuse suggested, can serve as a sort of gauge for a free society. He found a source for the form that a new society could take in the area of sensibility. Marcuse would argue, however, that sensibility is formed from the conditions of the social structure as well as from the explicit and rational data of the world. He would further argue that sensibility and rationality can only be transformed by engaging in praxis, the collective practice of creating an environment.

It is not clear where this leaves Marcuse. On the one hand, he appears to assume some biological base for sensibility; and, on the other hand, he appears to see new sensibility as emerging from new social conditions. I strongly suspect that Marcuse has, at least as a sensibility of his own, a basic idea of the "good man" grounded in his biology. If freed, it could redirect the formation of a rational world.

The importance here of Marcuse's position is the recognition of an area of sensibility or aesthetic rationality. The dual dialectic of inner aesthetic and technical rationality and outer individual and social condition is implicit in his statements. The difference between our views would apparently be the poverty of sources of aesthetic rationality that he appears to accept and the necessity of treating sensibility only in the context of the construction of new social environments. I propose that there are phenomenologically identifiable sources of aesthetic rationality not accounted for by Marcuse, and phenomenologically identifiable methods of creating individual perceptual environments and enlarging human sensibility that do not depend upon praxis as he defines it.

The problem of the source and validation of values is thus not adequately resolved in the ideologies described by Kohlberg and Mayer or by the radical position. We are left essentially with values that are either picked up culturally by association or conditioned in us behavioristically, emergent from our biological nature, or derived from cognitive reflection upon experience (individually or historically).

None of these approaches can account for the emergence, validation, and source of all values without ignoring a sizable segment of our own cultural history and personal experience. Values I would submit, as with knowledge, are personal, developed from a dual dialectical process that represents development in a hierarchical structure that surpasses one's biology, culture, or society.

Psychological theory, if there must be such an adjunct to educational ideology, must also be seen as a focus upon the question of human being. That is, narrow empirical or developmental views lead us away from our ontological ground of being rather than causing us to come to grips with human nature. They must also be grounded in something beyond their own conceptions. Thus, psychological theory must be grounded in existence and utilize the methods of phenomenology if it hopes to cope with being.

I have found much of value in the works of C. G. Jung[5] and William James.[6] The sense of their works for me lies in their apparent willingness to cope with all forms of psychological manifestation in human activity and to discipline their inquiries through observation and phenomenological methodology. I am less concerned with their conceptualizations than their orientation and methodology, although their concepts have been useful in many instances.

Jung was concerned with metaphysics throughout both his practical work and his theoretical writing. His biography is a rare experience in reading; it tells us that he was a fascinating, introspective, and idiosyncratic individual, but, more important, it shows how he used his personality in his work. He is perhaps a modern paradigm of man's unified struggle for meaning, using his own personality and culture and methodologically disciplining that inner struggle and cultural potential to probe the nature of human being.

As an analytical psychologist, he never developed a theory of child development. He felt that the ideas of Freud and Adler were perfectly usable with the young. Instead, he focused on the process of individuation, and it is the implications of this concept that contribute to the transcendental ideology of education.

Jung worked most often with people who were successful in life, but who, upon reaching middle age, found that life lacked meaning. He felt that the tasks of the first half of life were best symbolized by the myth of the hero. What concerned him was, as Anthony Storr says, what happened when the hero emancipated himself from the past, proved his (Adlerian) power, and gained his (Freudian) mate?

This led Jung and his patients to a search for values, and for Jung the supreme value was that of integration, of "wholeness." Thus, the conscious attitude of integration is one of acceptance, of ceasing to do violence to one's own nature by repressing or overdeveloping any part of it. This Jung called a "religious" attitude, although not necessarily related to any recognizable creed.

Then, the second half of life became a spiritual quest. He believed, contrary to Freud, that the concept of God was a "psyche aptitude" of human nature appearing everywhere in culture and history. He further believed that only by recognizing some higher authority than the ego could people detach themselves sufficiently from sexuality, the will to power, and other compulsions. If man had no spiritual inner experience, he would make a God of something else, whether sex, power, or even rationality. The God Jung discovered through his work was the sense of "wholeness," the undiscovered self.

The problem of alienation for Jung was an alienation from the ground of his being. Thereby it created loneliness, and his life lacked meaning and significance. Loneliness did not, he felt, come from having no people around; it came from being out of touch with oneself and thus being unable to communicate things that seem important or from holding views that others deem inadvisable.

Concepts that Jung used to express his views such as "archetypes," the "collective unconscious," his psychological typology of "introversion-extroversion," are more or less useful as the case may be. They are not central to my own thinking except to point toward an inner potential that the person must come to experience.

Of perhaps greater use is Jung's concept of the psyche being self-regulating. That, for Jung, was a psychology of "individuation" based upon the idea that the person is self-regulating when he has attained a balance and integration in his potentialities. Self-regulation strives toward unity, toward the integration of inner and outer realities in a meaningful wholeness.

James, on the other hand, was a self-proclaimed supernaturalist, in contrast to a naturalistic perspective of what he called a "crass" or pluralistic nature. He was, I suspect, as American as "apple pie" in his generally optimistic, searching, pluralistic, pragmatic, and radical empirical bent. Yet he was an unusual person for a psychologist because he had an insatiable curiosity about all the phenomena of human personal experience, and an aversion to closed or absolute meanings.

James felt as at home examining extrasensory perception or religious experiences as the more mundane aspects of attention, perception, cognition, and so forth. Jung refers to James's earlier work in a number of instances, but James probably died before he was well acquainted with Jung's work.

The lesson that James leaves us is similar to Jung's in that his openness and methodology reflect an attitude toward psychology that is especially useful for our purposes. What James brings to our thought is a more critical use of the dialectic between inner implicit and outer explicit reality. By acceptance of the inner realm as a source of meaning, James only intends that we test it in our lives, that we accept it as phenomenological fact but verify it for ourselves by its meaning for us in our human activity. It is, in other words, a dialectic of self-reflection of the commerce between our inner and explicit consciousness, and its verification for us (as in the case of psychoanalysis) does not necessarily invalidate or validate concretely the experiences of others or limit the potential of human beings.

Thus, for James, Jung's concepts might well be what James called "overbeliefs." What he would agree to is the critical acceptance of human experiences seemingly arising from within but central to the understanding of humanness. Thus, he could say, "Disregarding overbeliefs, and confining ourselves to what is common and generic, we have in the *fact that the conscious* person is continuous with a wider self through which . . . *experiences* come, a positive content of experience which, it seems to me, is *literally and objectively true as far as it goes.*"[7]

He concludes his work in religious experiences with his expression of his own overbelief, sounding somewhat like Carlos Castaneda and his adventures with Don Juan. "The whole drift of my education goes to persuade me that the world of our present consciousness is only one out of many worlds of consciousness that exist, and that those other worlds must contain experiences which have a meaning for life also; and that although in the main their experiences and those of this world keep discrete, yet the two become continuous at certain points, and higher energies filter in."[8]

Components of Epistemology

The epistemological components of a transcendental ideology are grounded in the concept of personal knowledge. Thus, knowledge is not simply things and relationships that are real in the outer world and waiting to be discovered, but it is a process of personalizing the outer world through the inner potential of the human being as it interacts with outer reality.

At this level I am speaking not of idiosyncratic individual worlds, although these are important, but I am referring to the idea that the created culture of human life is a common set of personal constructs. Personal in the sense that all cognitive constructs are grounded in individual personal meaning and that our shared culture, as well as language usages, serves as a pragmatic survival device. This outer necessity does not change the fundamental nature of knowledge.

The work of Michael Polanyi[9] is instructive at this point. He develops the idea of the tacit dimension of knowledge. By this I take him to mean that any explicit knowing is grounded in a tacit knowing that makes sense out of explicit statements. Thus, Polanyi begins with what he calls the fact "that we can know more than we can tell."

It is necessary to understand what one knows in order to make sense of it. Polanyi refers to this as a process of "indwelling." Understanding, however, is tacit in that understanding may only be inferred from the explicit knowledge we possess. This process of tacit knowing exists in both practical and formal knowledge structures, and in aesthetic and scientific realms.

As Polanyi remarks, "The skill of a driver cannot be replaced by a thorough schooling in the theory of the motorcar: The knowledge I have of my own body differs altogether from the knowledge of its physiology; and the rules of rhyming and prosody do not tell me what a poem told me, without any knowledge of its rules."[10] And, a mathematical theory can be constructed only by relying on prior tacit knowing and can function as a theory within an act of knowing, which consists in our attending from it to the previously established experience on which it bears.

Many of our present educational problems seem more understandable if we accept the tacit dimension of knowing. It is useful, for example, to consider the problem of school achievement among culturally different populations as fundamentally a problem of tacit knowing.

In Polanyi's terms, explicit knowledge use requires an act of commitment that cannot be formalized since "you cannot express a commitment noncommitally." The lack of commitment among culturally different students has been referred to as motivation and attention or value problems. Essentially it can be thought of as the absence of a tacit knowing which makes sense of (helps the student understand) the meaning of the explicit knowledge he is encountering. In mundane terms he lacks the experiential background for the tasks. He has not interiorized experiences that make sense of his school tasks. Thus, he is unable to *understand* and *commit* himself to the enterprise.

On a more general level, the problems of testing take on a more understandable quality when seen in the light of tacit knowledge. The sense of injustice and unfairness encountered frequently among students in reference to tests is helpfully explained when one accepts the idea that "we can know more than we can tell" and that it is possible not to understand the meaning or direction of tests and err because the tacit awareness we bring to a test situation may well not match the tacit assumption of the test maker.

A positive side to this problem may be seen in the use of humor. Much of our humor in the form of stories is grounded in the development of a story line that arouses a tacit understanding in the listener and is revealed to be in error when the punch line is delivered. The punch line is frequently "funny" because the listener quickly realizes that the tacit base in the story has been juxtaposed to his own tacit knowledge. A good humorist is a past master of utilizing the tacit dimension.

An epistemology must further come to grips with the so-called hard knowledge of our culture. It seems doubtful if any knowledge is "harder" than modern physics, and it is instructive to note epistemological implications found in the knowledge of modern physical science.

According to Arthur Koestler[11] modern physics has entered a phase of epistemology whereby modern physicists are ever more receptive to the possibility of the seemingly impossible. In a way one might say, at least in relation to the subatomic or supergalactic dimension, that physicists have literally gone out of their senses.

According to Koestler, Werner Heisenberg, in the field of quantum physics, has remarked that "atoms are not things . . . when we get down to the atomic level, the objective world of space and time no longer exists, and the mathematical symbols of theoretical physics refer merely to possibilities, not to facts." The Principle of Uncertainty or Indeterminacy, credited to Heisenberg, demonstrates that the more accurately a physicist is able to determine the velocity of an electron, the less able he is to determine its location (and the reverse).

Further, matter as entity behaves as waves or particles, but on mutually exclusive terms. This concept of complementarity means that two mutually exclusive frames of reference are complementary. Both are needed to provide an exhaustive view of phenomena.

As Sir James Jeans[12] said, "Today there is a wide measure of agreement, which on the physical side of science approaches almost to unanimity, the stream of knowledge is heading toward a non-mechanical reality; the universe begins to look more like a great thought than like a great machine."

The story of neutrinos is perhaps the most bewildering. Neutrinos, it appears, have virtually no physical properties and apparently pass through solid bodies as if they were empty space. Koestler further tells how V. A. Firsoff described neutrons as existing in a different kind of space, governed by different laws.

There is, of course, much more to modern physical theory, but it is a journey that I am ill prepared to take. I can only relate what reporters in this field seem to feel the knowledge implications are. In essence, the materialistic cause-effect world has collapsed as explanation of newly perceived phenomena. These phenomena appear to operate in a different dimension of reality and are referred to by many in mentalistic rather than materialistic terms.

Koestler, in his work, sees a convergence between physical theory and the data of extrasensory perception. At least the findings and theories of modern physicists are no less "unusual" and tend to be partially integratable with such things as precognition and psychokinesis. Fundamentally, he feels they reveal a basic polarity in matter which he describes as causal self-assertive tendency and an acausal integration tendency to function as a part of a larger whole. He ends his essay with "the limitation of our biological equipment may condemn us to the role of Peeping Toms at the keyhole of eternity. But at least let us take the stuffing out of the keyhole, which blocks even our limited view."[13]

An article by Bilanvik and Sudarshan[14] further illustrates the incredible potential of emerging physical theory. They remark that there is an unwritten precept in modern physics that "anything which is not prohibited is compulsory." They then go on to attempt to demonstrate that in terms of relativity theory there is no contradictory reason why "negative energy particles" traveling "backward in time" cannot exist. In the process they posit the existence of what they name "transcendent" tachyons.

An epistemology that does not recognize tacit knowledge components, or the fantastic possibilities and implications of our most advanced fields of inquiry, is simply weighted down with the baggage of philosophical and materialistic biases. How, what, and why are far more open questions than we are often led to believe, and the possibilities of accessibility to knowledge from "hidden" inner sources operating on acausal, or integrative, or serial and synchronistic bases point directly toward the awareness of another ground of knowledge in human being.

Centering as the Aim of Education

The aim of education should be a centering of the person in the world. Mary Caroline Richards[15] has expressed this idea beautifully. Much of what I have to say is at least consonant with her views, if not directly adapted from them.

Centering does not mean mental health. Though I have no quarrel with the intentions of people who want everyone to be mentally healthy, the term is too ridden with a psychologism that limits our perspective about human beings. It appears as a statistical concept, and those who are mentally healthy may in fact be "other-directed" persons, having little sense of a core or center.

Further, centering does not mean self-actualization, for that process, at least as I interpret it, is filled with assumptions about personality development that seem arbitrary and somewhat closed to me. One's personality, I would feel, is better thought of as something to be used to find a centering rather than something to be developed. Our efforts are better spent helping personalities as we find them ground their selves in a center of their being.

The idea of centering may be found in a wide variety of sources throughout history and the contemporary world. It is essentially what William James called a religious experience, although here it seems more appropriate to refer to the *spiritual.*

It is important that centering be recognized as a process that may occur in a religious context, but it is not dependent upon any sect or creed, whether Eastern Zen or Western Christianity, for its validation. It is a human experience facilitated in many ways by a religious attitude when this attitude encompasses the search to find our inner being or to complete one's awareness of wholeness and meaning as a person.

The work of some psychologists is important in helping us recognize the existence of inner potential, but the science of psychology, with its methodological and assumptive base, can only point toward the existence of the experience of centering. It cannot deal directly with it.

The "back door" or "front door" of human being, whichever suits your purpose, must be unlocked and left ajar if centering is to occur. The process draws its power and energy from sources that are not completely explicable. The naming of these sources of energy is not terribly helpful, even though one word that occurs frequently in relation to this experience is God. But God is not known; He is not understood; He is used. Thus, centering occurs through the use of spiritual resources, whatever one wishes to call them.

Spiritual energy does not shape the explicit knowledge of the person in absolute or noncultural ways. Centering takes place within the culture of the individual, and the process of centering utilizes the data of an individual's culture, what he explicitly knows through social praxis. The variety of religions, mystics, spiritualists, and other manifestations found throughout history fundamentally tells us that inner resources and strength can be made available and used but not what verbal form or perceptual reality this potential takes.

Centering as the aim of education calls for the completion of the person or the creation of meaning that utilizes all the potential given to each person. It in no way conflicts with the accumulated knowledge of a culture; it merely places this knowledge in the base or ground from which it grows. As such, centering is the fundamental process of human being that makes sense out of our perceptions and cognitions of reality.

It is important we do not turn away from examining the idea of centering simply because it is connected with spirituality. This term simply is the best one available in the attempt to refocus our fundamental educational concerns, even though it is fraught with heavy cultural biases in our society.

The data of spiritual literature when related to the axiological, psychological, social, and epistemological components I have alluded to make it quite difficult for us to reject the possibilities of centering. It appears to me that we are witnessing a period of discovery and transition leading toward a convergence of phenomena very much like centering. I, personally, am satisfied with the particular term.

What kinds of questions can we now ask about curriculum in view of the developmental aim of centering?

1. What kinds of activity are encouraged that provide for opening up perceptual experiences?
2. What kinds of activity facilitate the process of sensitizing people to others, to inner vibrations?
3. What kinds of activity provide experiences for developing close-knit community relationships?

4. What kinds of activity encourage and facilitate religious experiences?
5. What kinds of activity facilitate the development of patterned meaning structures?
6. What ways can we organize knowledge to enlarge human potential through meaning?
7. How can we facilitate the development of inner strength and power in human beings?

CURRICULUM CONTENT

Let me take a mundane example of the implications of the perspective of centering on the so-called discipline by focusing upon mathematics. Then we can reflect on more speculative but less mundane matters.

It is apparent that the substance of the culture we call discipline may be used to create new knowledge to be passed on, to provide substantive content within social roles to attack social problems, or to enlarge individual human potential.

If we were fundamentally concerned about enlarging human potential, we would view mathematics as a way of conceptualizing or thinking and creating a special kind of meaning system. Being able to think mathematically would result in the development of a human potential that could not be gained through any other avenue. Mathematics, in other words, could be seen as a special world perspective, not as a single view but one of a number of potential cultural views for opening up individuals to their potential.

This is counterposed to, though not mutually exclusive from, either the language use of mathematics for creating science, or pure mathematics, or the functional uses of computation. Teaching mathematics "for its own sake" means for the sake of enlarging the human potential of individuals in a way that is unique.

The importance of this perspective may be referred back to the developmental point of view provided by Kohlberg and Mayer. If we accept Dewey's concept of providing experiences that both interest people and contribute to their long-range development, it is clearly essential that the kind of long-range development be identifiable. Is the long-range development to be seen in terms of the discipline of mathematics? Or is it to be viewed in terms of its social usefulness to the individual in society? Or is it to be oriented toward the development of potential patterns of meaning for individuals?

Though, as I said, these ends are not mutually exclusive, they are functionally different in the sense that, when we make educative value judgments about the kinds and patterns of experiences people encounter, we create a situation which in practice reflects one of these orientations as a primary view of the goal of development.

What is problematical about mathematics? If we assume, for lack of a better term, that a desirable mathematical problem for an individual is one which he sees as problematic and which promises to contribute to his long-range development, does it make any difference how we help him to create experiences that will meet both criteria in terms of one or another of the possible long-range perspectives? I think that it clearly does make a fundamental difference in the way we create curriculum environments and the manner in which we enter into instructional practices.

It is very difficult for me to see exactly what kinds of experiences would facilitate the long-range development of meaning perspective through mathematics. I can only alert mathematicians or mathematical thinkers to this task. But I think that I can clearly see some things we presently do that do not contribute directly to this end.

It makes no sense to me from this view, for example, to have a highly sequenced, logically programmed mathematics curriculum. The kind of mathematics and when it is encountered must be based upon a far more sensitive awareness of the meaning systems of individuals. Further, it makes little sense to structure the great majority of learning tasks in a convergent manner. It would appear to me that "playing" with numbers in a much freer kind of problem situation would be far more valuable.

Nor does it make much sense to "package" mathematics textbooks and other materials around narrow tasks, skills, or computations. It would be far better to set out to create mathematics as a set of problem situations that can be entered at different levels by different persons who can then branch out, if they wish, into geometry, algebra, calculus, or what have you. Thus, the emphasis upon individuated entrance in mathematical meaning systems, open and playful encounters, and highly diverse materials built around a problem situation that can go in a variety of directions sounds much more satisfying to me.

Ecology is an emerging social concern that has a corollary in the centering process. It takes a unitary view of the world. Thus, the inner unity of the centering process has an outer reality in the concern for a unitary world built upon an understanding of ecology. It appears that any sane attempt to educate the young must deal substantively with the impact of man and technology on his own living environment, and there appears to be little hope that we can simply solve our ecological problems with the next generation of technological developments. Ecological problem solutions call for the same value search and commitment growing from the inner knowledge of what we are and what we can be. There is a need to transcend the linear and technical problem-solving approaches of the past if we are to survive our ecological crises. Thus, a global view of the interrelationships of human structures and activities must be a central aspect of any curriculum which purports to have a transcendent developmental view.

This section on content can be concluded with one last reflection that I owe to Charity James, with whom I worked for a year at Goldsmith College at the University of London. If we were intent upon developing human potential, we would realize that we live in a highly verbal, conceptual culture. We would further realize, as Lawrence Kubie[16] has pointed out, that we tend to pay a high price in potential for this human achievement. The price is fundamentally related to the dialectic of our explicit and inner selves, and it is focused upon the withering away of portions of our creative potential. This is not new, but what is rarely noted is that the emphasis upon nonverbal or body language, hidden culture, or the arts, is not crucial in this matter.

What we seem to lose is our ability to gain access to ourselves and our creative potential through the process of visualization. We have in fact created a negative concept called hallucinations to guard against the very use of some of the visualizing potential. We seem not to trust ourselves.

Dreams are, I suppose, a human example of the process of visualization, yet dreams are rarely in our control. What I speak of is the power to control and create visualization, to bring to our vision things not present to our senses. To have visions is not the same as to create them.

A somewhat dramatic illustration of the human potential for visualization is provided by Colin Wilson[17] in his biography of Abraham Maslow. Wilson was lecturing in one of Maslow's classes when he remarked that in the human act of masturbation it is possible by imagination to carry on a sexual activity where the mental act needs no object.

Maslow objected and pointed out that monkeys also masturbate. Wilson responded with the question of whether Maslow (whose early work was in the primate laboratory at Wisconsin) had ever seen a male monkey masturbate in total isolation, without the stimulus of a female monkey somewhere in the vicinity. Maslow remarked that he had not. Thus, Wilson illustrated the capacity of the human being to make a physical response via visualization as if to reality.

The Processes in Curriculum

Centering is the aim of a transcendental ideology. As such, it is a process one enters into. Thus, the question of the objectives of a transcendental curriculum must be seen in process terms also. But processes are not ends in themselves. The ends are infinitely varied and unknowable in any finite sense with reference to a given individual. Processes, rather, refer to the engagement of the individual in human activity, which facilitates the process of centering.

For the sake of clarity an analogy may be made at this point to Dewey's developmental ideology. That is, if centering is viewed as the long-range developmental goal of curriculum, then process and content may be seen in terms of this goal. Content is selected in terms of the readiness and interest level of the students, primarily by the person involved coming to know what their immediate concerns are that are related to cultural substance. The essential component remains the processes or activities or events that occur. There are a number of possible processes that would facilitate centering.

Pattern making. This critical process reflects itself in the need to transform reality symbolically, to create order in search of meaning, and it is fundamental for locating oneself in time and space and for providing cognitive awareness that may facilitate centering. The pattern making process must be distinguished clearly from the transmission of preformed patterns to the individual. Although cultural substance can never be formless by definition, the emphasis placed upon the nature of the individual encounter is critical. Thus, pattern making would emphasize the creative and personal ordering of cultural data as the individual engaged in activity.

Playing. The attitude and activity of play is a critical aspect of the pattern-making process. Play in this sense refers to playing with ideas, things, and other people. To engage in the encounter with cultural substance in a playful manner provides the individual with a self-regulating potentiality. Playfulness is at the service of the individual and frees persons to order and create without the necessity of constant attention and direction of the adult world. Thus, the process of "playing" would seem to be necessary to facilitate pattern making and to provide for self-regulation of activity.

Meditative thinking. "Why" is the fundamental thought question for a transcendental ideology, why in the sense of examining the fundamental meaning of things. Technical or calculative thinking, so central to our society, is built into the very pores of our social skin. To facilitate centering in the individual we must encourage meditative thinking. Rather than fostering the activity of thought in a functional, utilitarian way, a problem-solving process, we must foster what Martin Heidegger[18] called a "releasement toward things" and an "openness to the mystery." Thus, nothing can be accepted simply on its own terms in its social utility. Rather, we must encourage the young to say both yes and no to culture and probe the ground from which our culture arises, through meditative thinking.

Imagining. Another way of approaching pattern making, play, and meditative thinking comes through the activity of imagining—imagining as a process in contrast to verbalizing. Our verbal culture and language culture and language forms, as useful and necessary as they are, have also become the dominant form of thinking and expressing ourselves. The danger of this one-sided verbal emphasis is the constant externalizing of meaning, of coming to name the object and manipulate external reality. Imagining on the contrary provides an internal referent for the external world. The work of Rudolf Steiner[19] and the Waldorf Schools provides considerable insight into this process. Steiner emphasizes the technique of presenting knowledge to the child first through his own imagination and only later following up with empirical observation. In essence the individual first forms his own images of encounters as he listens or actively creates. Thus, imagination as the ability to picture in the mind what is not present to the senses is a perceptual power that involves the whole person, that puts him in contact with the ground of his being.

The aesthetic principle. It is clear that the guidance of much of the arrangement of physical facilities, interpersonal relations, and individual expression must come from what Herbert Read[20] called the aesthetic principle. Read called the guidance of human education by the aesthetic principle the natural form of education. The preadolescent education of individuals, Read argued, should move from feeling to drama, sensation to visual and plastic design, intuition to dance and music, and thought to craft. Then, from the play of children emerging from their feelings, sensations, intuitions, and thinking, the individual could gradually grow toward cultural art forms guided by the aesthetic principle. Thus, the activities of dramatization, designing, dancing, playing music, and making or crafting are important in a transcendent ideology.

The body and our biology. Physical education, Alan Watts[21] has said, is "the fundamental discipline of life." Watts, however, did not mean the games and skills of the traditional curriculum. Rather, he meant coming to grips with our own biological being and all that it means. Thus, he was able to propose that learning to husband plants and animals for food, how to cook, how to make clothes and build houses, how to dance and breathe, how to do yoga for finding one's true center, and how to make love were examples of this discipline. Although we rarely admit to a mind-body separation on a philosophical level, it is clear by the way we educate the young that we do not consider the biological aspects of the person to be relevant to the real business of education. Thus, the emphasis upon cognitive-verbal learning not only separates us from our inner resources but it divorces us from our biological organism. To be at home in our bodies is critical for human centering, and it would seem to me that far more attention should be paid to this phenomenon. It is interesting that the field of biofeedback is growing today. Thus, the use of machines to provide a conscious awareness of bodily functions, such as heartbeats or brain waves, may help to develop an integrated knowledge of the phenomena of our existence. It is perfectly reasonable to propose that the school curriculum processes may come to provide us with avenues for knowing ourselves as biological entities. Again, I would not claim biological and body knowledge as an end in itself. What I would say is that, in the centering of the human being, the awareness of "who I am" and "what my biological and physical potential are" are necessary avenues for the long-range development of the centering process.

The education of perception. This is the final area that needs exploring here. I refer to perception in the sense of William James's many other worlds of consciousness that exist aside from our present one, rather than in the sense of a functional psychological mechanism. The most impressive and exciting recent work in this area comes from an anthropologist—Carlos Castaneda's[22] fascinating trilogy, in which he relates his experiences with the old Indian medicine man. I am not sure what the implications of this work are, but I am sure that the creation of altered states of consciousness is a human potential that is important to the process of centering.

THE TEACHER IN THE PROCESS

The developmental ideology of Dewey, Piaget, and others, as described by Kohlberg and Mayer perceives the teacher to be a person who comes to know the students but who also makes judgments about the long-range implications of experiences on the development of the children. So far as this goes, then, it is not incompatible with a transcendental developmental ideology. A transcendental ideology would, however, define this process in a different manner.

The teacher from a transcendental point of view is also in process. That is, the developmental aim of centering is as valid and important to the person of the teacher as it is to the child. Thus, the teacher does not "stand back" in a judgmental stance in the same manner. Rather, the teacher is immersed in the process of centering from her own point of view. Thus, the relationships between students and teachers are mutually responsive to the aim of centering.

The key distinction between these two developmental ideologies is the fundamental difference between knowing and understanding. In a secular or psychological developmental ideology, knowing the child, knowing his developmental status, and knowing the long-range developmental goals are essentially explicit cognitive acts. They are dependent upon being once removed from the children in a judgmental stance. This implies a maturity that is static in its essence, an end point which only the teacher has access to and only the teacher has arrived at. Thus, the predominant rationality of the teacher is still a technical process of planning, manipulating, and calculating, even though the intentions and relationships are, for example, more humane, perhaps, than those found in cultural transmission ideology. A transcendental ideology would shift the predominant rationality toward the aesthetic, intuitive, and spontaneous in the mutual process of centering.

Children learning and teachers teaching are fundamentally dependent upon the tacit dimensions. Explicit awareness or knowledge of each other and of teaching or learning tasks is embedded in a tacit realm that provides the ground for understanding, for making activity meaningful. Teachers cannot be said to understand children simply because they possess a considerable amount of explicit knowledge about them. Understanding is a deeper concept. It demands a sort of indwelling in the other, a touching of the sources of the other. Understanding others is not a "useful" procedure in the sense that knowing is, in that it does not provide the basis for planning, manipulating, and calculating. Understanding provides the ground for relating, for being fully there in the presence and as a presence to the other, for what Huebner called a continuance of the joint pilgrimage. The explicit knowledge of child development or of specific children may facilitate our understanding of them if it is internalized and integrated into our inner self. It is, however, only one avenue toward understanding.

There is another path, much harder but more direct. This is the process of locating one's center in relation to the other: to "see" one's self and the other in relation to our centers of being; to touch and be touched by another in terms of something fundamental to our shared existence.

This act of relationship, called understanding, is only known after the fact. "*Now, I understand!*" It is an act of listening, but not to the explicit content that a person is expressing. Rather, it is "tuning in" to the "vibrations" of bodily rhythms, feeling tone, inward expressions of a person's attempts to integrate and to maintain his integrity as a whole person.

Explicit content may facilitate this process, but often it creates a cognitive dissonance, an interference with really listening to the center of the person. We can easily be led away from this center by the way in which the other's explicitness reflects upon our own needs for centering. This interference raises barriers in ourselves to understanding, and shuts down our own expression of our being. So much of the explicit expression of cognition is really no more than dignified "cocktail chatter." Whether it is the weather, religion, sex education, politics, another person's foibles and problems, or the latest gossip does not matter.

Dialogue is different. Explicit cognitive expressions are oriented in dialogue toward creating something from the inner resources of two or more people. It is entered into with the intent of listening, and listening beneath the surface. The hope is that out of the explicit dialogue the creative inner workings of the participants will be freed and combined. Short of dialogue, even the expression of ideas, of philosophical or religious truths, of psychological insights, is often in the service of the cognitive ego of the participants. Dialogue does not just occur in a face-to-face relation; it can take place for the person through reading a book, or even, heaven forbid, listening to a talk on curriculum theory. Inner verbal and visual activities are possible without direct interaction.

Problem solving as a vehicle for progressive interactive method in this context, on the other hand, necessitates the introduction of social power structures in order to facilitate activity. Thus, when development is based upon a problem-solving schema, the orientation of activity is externalized, and it necessitates the organization of human activity into a social power structure. It further implies that development is a process of mastering the outer world through solutions by problem-solving methods of intelligence. When centering is the main process in relationships, problems are not always solved. As centering evolves, some problems disappear, still others become redefined, and some are solved in a sense of bringing to bear unity of self through thought, feeling, and action.

Psychoanalysis, one supposes, is a recognition of the phenomena of inner meaning in each person. Yet, as valuable as the process may be, the difference in the ability of psychologists to help others lies mainly in their ability to listen and understand, not in terms of their cognitive developmental theories but in interpreting the explicit data of the other as symbolic or in getting individuals to solve their own problems. The successful psychoanalyst is probably one who listens and reveals his own centeredness, who helps the patient gather his own inner resources for centering by being and revealing, by listening and responding, by offering and receiving.

Implicit understanding is to poetry as explicit knowledge is to science. The explicitness of science is in contrast to the unity and expressiveness of poetry. Science "adds up"; poetry integrates. It is becoming less clear to scientists whether explicit knowledge even "adds up," not at least until we have made a poem of the other in our own being. When we make a poem of the other in ourselves, we do not trap either in categories and classes. When we understand each other, we create a shared poem of our existence. Understanding is the crystallization of our aesthetic knowing; explicit knowledge is its rational handmaiden. To know a child is to describe his characteristics; to understand him is to be able to write a poem that captures his essence.

The teacher in such a process is, therefore, engaged in the art of living. The task of both student and teacher is the development of their own centering through contact with culture and society, bringing as much of their whole selves as they can to bear upon the process. There is no specifiable set of techniques or of rules or of carefully defined teaching roles. It is primarily a willingness to "let go" and to immerse oneself in the process of living with others in a creative and spontaneous manner, having faith in ourselves, others, and the culture we exist in as a medium for developing our own centering.

In concluding, I would like to clear up one possible misconception about the processes of curriculum and teaching leading toward centering in the educational ideology of transcendence. These processes are not haphazard; nor do they operate upon the romantic notion of the natural unfolding of the child. I quote from Mary Caroline Richards:

It is a terrible thing when a teacher gives the impression that he does not care what the child does. It is false and it is unfaithful. The child hopes that an adult will have more sense and more heart than that. The teacher therefore seeks to understand what the child hungers for in the life of his imagination, his mind, his senses, his motion, his will. This means that he (the teacher) does not take things at their face value, but sees elements in relation to a lifetime process of deep inner structure.[23]

NOTES

1. Lawrence Kohlberg and Rochelle Mayer, "Development As the Aim of Education," *Harvard Educational Review* 42, No. 4 (November 1972), 449-96.

2. Paulo Freire, *Pedagogy of the Oppressed* (New York: Herder and Herder, 1970), p. 186.

3. Peter Berger, *A Rumor of Angels* (Garden City, New York: Doubleday Anchor Book, 1969), p. 103.

4. Herbert Marcuse, *An Essay on Liberation* (Boston: Beacon Press, 1969), p. 91, and *One Dimensional Man* (Boston: Beacon Press, 1964).

5. C. G. Jung, *The Basic Writings of C. G. Jung,* ed. V. S. De Lazlo (New York: Modern Library, 1959), p. 544.

6. William James, *Varieties of Religious Experiences,* (New York: New American Library, 1958), p. 396; John Wild, *The Radical Empiricism of William James* (Garden City, New York: Doubleday Anchor Book, 1970), p. 420.

7. James, *Varieties of Religious Experiences,* p. 388.

8. *Ibid.,* p. 391.

9. Michael Polanyi, *The Tacit Dimensions* (Garden City, New York: Doubleday Anchor Book, 1967), p. 99.

10. *Ibid.,* p. 20.

11. Arthur Koestler, *The Roots of Coincidence* (New York: Random House, 1972), p. 158.

12. Sir James Jeans, *The Mysterious Universe* (Cambridge, Eng.: Cambridge University Press, 1937), p. 172.

13. Koestler, *Roots of Coincidence,* p. 140.

14. Olexa-Myron Bilanvik and E. C. George Sudarshan, "Particles beyond the Light Barrier," *Physics Today* (May 1969), 43-51.

15. Mary Caroline Richards, *Centering* (Middletown, Connecticut: Wesleyan University Press, 1962), p. 159.

16. Lawrence Kubie, "Protecting Preconscious Functions," in *Nurturing Individual Potential,* A.S.C.D., the Association, 1963.

17. Colin Wilson, *New Pathways in Psychology* (New York: Taplinger Publishing Co., 1972), p. 289.

18. Martin Heidegger, *Discourse on Thinking,* Harper Torchbook (New York: Harper and Row, 1966), p. 93.

19. Rudolf Steiner, *The Essentials of Education* (London: Rudolf Steiner Publishing Co., 1968).

20. Herbert Read, *Education through Art* (London: Faber and Faber, 1956), p. 308.

21. Alan Watts, *In My Own Way* (New York: Pantheon Books, 1972).

22. E.g., Carlos Castaneda, *Journeys with Don Juan* (New York: Simon and Schuster, 1969).

23. Richards, *Centering,* pp. 101-102.

VII. IN THE STILLNESS IS THE DANCING

William F. Pilder

THINGS FALL APART

Heightened consciousness and cultural revolution tend to run together though the phrases are a bit weighty and carry too many negative whispers. They point to the excitement of this time and space, its adventure, romance, and pain. At the deepest level of my self and those I love, strange but wonderful things are happening—seeing things never seen before, losing what before seemed so essential, finding that a sense of loss can also be accompanied by a sense of release. Out of these personal revolutions there is a seeking of reconciliation with work, wanting professional expression to be self-expression. Here the tension begins. Somehow places of work do not accommodate the new personal desires, and the frustration gives rise to a painful, freeing discovery: there is no reconciliation with dying structures. New wine in old wineskins means waste, spilling of the precious.

To be specific, I no longer hope to relate curriculum theory to major upheavals occurring in people at the level where culture resides. Culture is not out there somewhere; culture is where we live, the place of our indwelling. To express culture in work demands a shared way of living, a mutual indwelling. This mutuality is precisely what is absent in places of work today. Every institution making up the social fabric has ceased to be a place where those within can work together because they share a common ground. Curriculum thinking has always assumed this common ground, so after determining mechanically what society, the learner, and the disciplines required, decisions were made about what to do. Such a process can result in the worst kind of violence toward some. Not everybody wants to live the same way, which is what consciousness means—visions, cracks in the egg, alternate realities. Yet one man's vision may or may not be shared, so there is no curriculum to be made from a vision. Consciousness is what is lived; it is more than can be told. In the reflections that follow I want to keep separate consciousness and curriculum theory. They have fallen apart for me, and all the king's horses and all the king's men will never put Humpty together again.

THE DEMISE OF THE PROGRESSIVE DREAM

The falling apart is a scaling down of expectations, the end of the progressive dream. The time is now to stop thinking and talking about using curricula in schools to accomplish major social change. The time is now to begin living the changes, and dialogue needs to occur about this living. Schools can return to readin', writin', and 'rithmetic.

Participation in the depths of what is occurring at the level of consciousness is imperative if the globe is to survive, but schools have little to do with that survival. The inevitable myopia of professional points of view, forgivable in times of cultural stability, is unforgivable when man is threatened from both without and within. To meet the threat that is upon us, nothing less than conversion is necessary. I use the word carefully, stressing its root meaning: a turning around. The values underlying both capitalist and communist systems must be turned around, but to use the schools to accomplish this would be to make the same error now being made.[1] The schooling process now turns the spirit to serve social values hell bent on global destruction. There is no way to employ that same process to achieve a new set of values; means and ends must both come out of new visions, new indwellings.[2] Keeping curriculum theory together with consciousness and cultural revolution can only perpetuate the illusion that something important is being done if school curricula are related to the latest happenings available in the media.[3]

THE SWAY AND STAGGER OF TRANSFORMATION

With these remarks as a preface, then, I would like to share my personal experience and reflections on what is happening with how I am in the world. Being alive today, I feel I am participating in a marvelous transformation taking place on a global scale. I am caught up in this transformation along with every person seeking to experience his present. To the extent that I can understand my own transformation, I believe I can begin to discern the nature of the cultural revolution in which I live. This revolution is a hope for me, a journey toward light, not darkness.

I am increasingly conscious of how much this is a time of living on the edge between hope and despair. I recently discovered Karl Barth's description of the ambivalence in which contemporary man exists: a swaying and staggering between "Yes" and "No."[4] In a time of decaying social structures and bankrupt symbols, there is so much to deny that the Yes can be lost. The trap of mere negation threatens constantly, and swaying and staggering characterize the journey.

The loss of the Yes is the sword of Damocles, the constant threat dangling overhead, the ever-present possibility of Kierkegaard's sickness unto death. More than anyone, Kierkegaard's formulation of the nature of consciousness and its relation to despair or mere negation captures for me the struggle of the present. For him, consciousness is consciousness of self.

Generally speaking, consciousness, i.e., consciousness of self, is the decisive criterion of the self. The more consciousness, the more self, the more consciousness, the more will, and the more will the more self. A man who has no will at all is no self; the more will he has, the more consciousness of self he has also.[5]

As consciousness increases, the possibility of saying only No likewise increases.

With every increase in the degree of consciousness, and in proportion to that increase, the intensity of despair increases: the more consciousness, the more intense the despair.[6]

The eradication of this despair, the holding on to the Yes, is the primary task of the present and is described by Kierkegaard in a formula that he later employs as the definition of faith.

This then is the formula which describes the condition of the self when despair is completely eradicated: by relating itself to its own self and by willing to be itself the self is grounded transparently in the Power which posited it.[7]

I do not know of a more apt description of the challenge of the present to every person seeking to heighten consciousness in order to participate fully in this moment of history. I want to work from the Kierkegaardian formula to further reflect on the specific forms participation is taking as the culture transforms itself.

Within Kierkegaard's formula is a tripartite relationship on which consciousness rests: self to self and the two elements of this relation in turn relating together to Another. Using other terms, I would describe this as the delicate balance between therapy and faith. Therapy involving the work of relating self to itself; faith entailing relating to Another experienced as a grounding, constituting Power.

THE TRIUMPH OF THE THERAPEUTIC

Philip Rieff's *The Triumph of the Therapeutic*[8] expertly details the nature of the therapeutic venture in the present. The subtitle of the book is "The Uses of Faith after Freud," and Rieff concludes that the man who triumphs in the present is one who needs no faith. Or, to point up the objectivist dilemma in which Rieff finds himself, his conclusion can be formulated as: The man who triumphs in the present is the man who has faith in the assertion that he needs no faith.[9] To be impaled on the horns of this dilemma is to experience a major aspect of the transformation of the culture. To fail to experience this dilemma, to feel it in the body, is to miss participating in the present.

Relating the self to itself is no easy matter in a culture that systematically erodes subjectivity. To know directly what I am feeling, to be in touch, to be grounded, and to be able to act directly out of this knowing is the result of constant effort. I have watched persons in various therapeutic contexts, group and individual, struggle for hours to reach a single emotion. The pain and frustration created in me as I watched makes me aware of how much I, too, am involved in the same struggle. Whatever the weaknesses of the popular therapeutic contexts available today, and they are many, they cannot be overlooked as significant efforts to enhance consciousness in a culture imprisoned in its head. Linear thinking, technological rationality, anomie, whatever label is used to describe the disease, part of the cure entails getting back to the body, relating self to self.

An increasing number of technologies are available to assist in this task of therapy. Gestalt, transaction analysis, bioenergetics, basic encounter are important theoretical points of view in which to participate. A caveat to keep in mind in the midst of participating in these technologies is their tendency to create chaotic subjectivity, anarchists in purely negative communities.[10] I believe it is deceptively easy to get stuck in this chaos. But being stuck is part of being on the road.

Within the therapeutic dimension of consciousness, chaos becomes a Satanic force, the exact reverse of the rigidity being opposed in outmoded cultural forms.

But the other side of the Devil, the exact reverse of his rigidity, is chaos. We know only too well by our own example, as individuals and as a whole, how this "other side" of our rigid consciousness looks. We engender within ourselves this structureless, blurred, impure amorphousness, this mass formlessness and aversion to form, wherever the Devil's rigidity dominates our consciousness and our life. The smooth, undifferentiated fixity of the one is inseparable from the molluscous, undifferentiated chaos of the other.[11]

The problem of form is central to the present cultural transformations because of the extent to which the negation of bankrupt forms has become necessary. Anyone who has worked at trying to create a learning context free of the deadly rigidities controlling compulsory, school-based learning, knows well the deadliness of formlessness. The vacuum engulfs every attempt to seriously transform an entrenched educational process, and in wrestling with this demon, some significant learning occurs. Still, forms that can be affirmed and asserted are essential. The complexity of creating forms in the present is that, in order for them to be adequate to their situation, they need to bring genuinely new matter to that situation. Rearranged old matter will not work.

Some examples that come to mind are free schools and alternative schools. The vacuum engulfs most free schools to the point of drowning, and so many alternative schools seem to be mere safety valves or spruced up versions of that same horrible machine. Both have been worthy efforts to assert new forms, but the substance from which the forms came lacked an essential newness.

I could be called to task for my own aversion to form in not wanting to connect curriculum theory with consciousness and cultural revolution. Yet in this context of discussing the problem of form, I feel certain that authentically new substance cannot be treated in the mode of a conference, and making curricula for schools out of talk about consciousness or cultural revolution is hopeless. I avidly hope for new cultural forms in which young and old can develop themselves, where they can learn from teachers they revere. I despair of any such forms emerging from contexts that do not create entirely new relationships.

Along with relating self to itself, Kierkegaard's description of consciousness also includes the idea of willing to be the self discovered in this process. Therapy so often stops with insight; all the problems are seen and can be deftly articulated, but life goes on as usual. Behavior need not change with insight, and the element of will becomes imperative. I believe the insights possible to any thinking person in the present about the quality of life demand radical changes in life style —new behaviors. Insight is cheap; new behaviors appear all too rare. I attribute this to lack of will in all of us.

Thus far I have considered the therapy dimension of Kierkegaard's description of consciousness. First, getting back in touch with the self, coming home, is work, given the culture that prevails. However, some important technologies are available to assist in this work, and lack of participation in these efforts indicates a cultural lag whether on the part of an individual or an institution. On the other hand, participation has its dangers, mainly that chaotic subjectivity results in a painful absence of form. This formlessness characterizes present efforts to transform learning contexts to be more consistent with the consciousness developed by therapeutic insights. Finally, insight without corresponding will to behave according to insight is impotent, and this impotence characterizes the cultural present.

ALTERNATE REALITIES AND BELIEF

The faith dimension of consciousness in the Kierkegaardian formula involves the experience of Another as a grounding, constituting Power. Here belief is presented as a firsthand experience of a Power within consciousness, not as a merely rational exercise in polemics, the acceptance or rejection of dry theological formulas. Kierkegaard points to an immanent Power, experienced as wholly Other but within the self. Tillich's metaphor, Ground of Being, likewise expresses this experience of immanence. Here the Power grounding the self is met within rather than experienced as outside or transcendent and this shift in consciousness is basic to the cultural transformations now taking place in the realm of belief.

Two most eloquent contemporary spokesmen for the experience of this inner Power which constitutes the self are Carlos Castaneda and John Lilly. Significantly, both men were initially involved as scientists in researching the effects of hallucinogenic drugs, the pursuit of which led to profound transformations. Their work produced basic changes in their way of life and how they viewed being a person within Western culture. Part of the future and the hope of this culture is in the direction that Castaneda and Lilly have begun to explore. Only the depth and completeness of the conversions they experienced can possibly meet the demands of the present on the human spirit. Unless masses of people begin living in alternative ways, the spiritual and ecological crisis cannot be met. Alternative life styles entail alternate views of reality.

From the point of view of phenomenology, reality is multiple. Both Castaneda and Lilly emphasize this view in their work. Castaneda refers to his apprenticeship with Don Juan as learning the praxis of phenomenology.[12] In *Center of the Cyclone,* Lilly stresses the power of mental programs over the reality that is or can be experienced.[13] These mental programs can actually be seen as programs, a certain inner space available to anyone who cares enough to get there, where the limitless Power of consciousness can be experienced. Within this space, alternate realities can be experienced and, after much struggle, integrated with consensus reality. This integration activity produces personal and cultural transformation and follows upon the direct, personal experience of alternate realities.

The struggle to integrate the profound personal experience of this inner Power that constitutes what we are and what we see characterizes the present for growing communities of people. The excitement of the present for me is involved in meeting growing numbers of pilgrims caught up in this struggle of integration.

The task of integration entails wrestling constantly with the temptation to withdraw from consensus reality to ensconce the self in the comfort and immense attraction of the alternate reality—dropping out or dropping in, depending on where I happen to be standing. Personally, I believe the tension between alternate and consensus reality views ought to be maintained. This tension is the primary source of cultural transformation, and the community is deprived of transformation energies when the tension is allayed in abandoning the consensus view by denial. The negative community is based on this type of denial and bears witness to the power of alternate reality visions. I judge this aspect of its power to be demonic, sucking the self into that self-created fire that consumes but gives off no warmth.

Like the demonic twins of chaos and rigidity described in considering the therapeutic dimension of consciousness, the struggle of faith today entails contending with the demons of withdrawal and identification. Withdrawal constantly entices the self toward mere denial as a means of allaying tension between personal vision and the world as it is. Identification relieves the tension by succumbing to all the social expectations that bombard the self by way of the political economy of images designed to destroy the soul.[14] The simplistic dichotomy of labels like freak or organization man prowls the consciousness with pointed tail, pitchfork, and Satanic grin. The dance of faith takes place on a tightrope stretching between these alternatives. Of course, the dance does not even begin without the experience of inner space where alternate realities can be glimpsed, and the way in is eminently personal. All anyone needs to begin is desire. The amount of desire around is the hope of the future.

The faith dimension of consciousness as described by Kierkegaard takes specific form in the present concern with alternate realities. The development of this dimension involves a journey inward and a subsequent struggle to integrate what is seen with how the self relates with consensus reality. Integration is constantly threatened by temptation toward withdrawal or identification. The tension of remaining in the middle is the primary source of creative transformation for the person and the culture.

ACHIEVING THE ZERO POINT

The development of consciousness depends, then, on a delicately balanced relationship between the two dimensions of therapy and faith. Though I have described these dimensions separately, they should be seen as dimensions of the same reality. Kierkegaard's formula is intended to describe a single reality that he names consciousness or faith, depending on his context. The separation of these dimensions occurs in a number of contexts today to the detriment of the participants. Research recently available on the impact of encounter groups stresses the negative effects of merely working at experiencing previously unseen emotion, relating self to self as cathartic release with little or no effort at the creation of meaning.

The most effective groups were those where meaning attribution was a strong component of the experience, that is, where the group leader made a consistent effort to give ideas or values to group members relating to the experience.[15] Such meaning attribution depends on a faith in the source of emotions previously repressed that now threaten to overwhelm. This faith constitutes an acceptance of such emotion as basically positive in origin and destination, as part of the self that is acceptable in spite of being unacceptable.[16] Such faith is not an automatic part of intensive group experiences, but it can be a quiet presence, depending on the leader.

Separating belief in a constituting Power from deep, personal, individual experience likewise creates destructive contexts. Movements of all kinds that demand submerging personal experience with a correlative disregard for persons separate from the movement haunt the present. There is a magic about such causes since they seem to offer intense meaning in the midst of collapsing personal meaning. The effort of constantly creating meaning as an individual can apparently be short circuited by participation in group meaning. Collective, communal effort is essential to the present, but such efforts must rest on the dignifying, not the denigration, of personal experience.

Keeping together these two dimensions of therapy and faith is the central task of consciousness development for the present. A new mode of knowing, personal and organic, can begin to pervade the culture if the task is accomplished. The prevailing culture is controlled by a process of knowing best described as impersonal and mechanistic, that powerful posture that produced the incredible reality of overkill. The monstrosity of overkill and similar threats to global survival can be met only by conversion to this new mode of knowing to the point where major social institutions are affected. The complexity of the present threat is that part of any solution demands the conversion of persons at the level of seeing and knowing reality. Social programs directed at institutions will not touch this part of the problem. Similarly, movements seeking converts to this new mode of knowing are an obvious self-contradiction—means belie ends.

Here, then, is my despair as a professional: human survival cannot depend on social programs directed at present institutional structures. Personal consciousness development and subsequent cultural transformation cannot be programmed in mechanistic fashion; a curriculum for consciousness development and cultural change is a blatant contradiction. From the ashes of this despair a Phoenix stirs —a single hope. The process that brings me to this loss of confidence in programs, in professional reality, in views of all kinds is a wave of transformation in my personal life and in the culture at large. This is my hope: a kind of zero point, a carefully held indifference between the contraries of identification with professional expectations and withdrawal inside a self-process. I try to walk the tightrope between rigidity and chaos and dance between the demons of professional identification and selfish withdrawal.

FOOD FOR THE PHOENIX

The important task now is to nourish the Phoenix of hope, protecting it from the loss of energy caused by alien, hostile surroundings, from what Reich called the "emotional plague." The task demands fidelity to my organism as a whole, to the subtle clues telling me whether I am standing in a place where the energy nourishes me or whether I need to walk away from forces that destroy. And though walking away may be interpreted as retreat, only I know what that still, small voice within demands for the long march ahead. Throughout the journey I must resist that perverse tendency to make normative what is simply my own pilgrimage, but at the same time I know that the only hold I have on truth is this sense of what I must do.

In concluding these reflections on personal consciousness and cultural transformation, I would like to share a recent experience that reflects in microcosm what I see occurring more widely in these two realms. A conference was held in Bloomington on the theme of "Indiana Tomorrow" in an effort to stimulate some thinking and promote relationships centered on creating a more attractive future. The intent of the conference was to combine the best of the voices in the field of technological forecasting with those pleading convincingly for a qualitatively different future, then to see where such a combination as input might lead a group of concerned persons from a spectrum of professions in Indiana. The Club of Rome study, *The Limits To Growth,*[17] provided a set of information relating to the global crisis from a systems analysis perspective replete with computer projections. Theodore Roszak's *Where the Wasteland Ends*[18] was a voice calling for personal change and the transcending of the myth of objective consciousness in order to achieve the necessary conversion of man, the reversal or apocatastasis. The Roszak vision was expressed in very personal terms by a young man who currently heads some sixteen ashrams in the midwest, where the teachings of Swami Rudrananda are studied and lived. The final input was from an expert on public policy and the management of bureaucracies reflecting on problems to be met for future social well-being.

Hours of effort to create some sense of direction for the future and for development, given these inputs, left the participants fatigued and hopeless about meaningful social action. Much effort was expended in refuting the position expressed by the leader of the ashrams as an indifferent, self-centered, myopic approach to social welfare. Frequently, the leaders of this refutation, whose position became characterized as activist, would in turn be chided by the resident systems analyst for their own myopia and mere symptomatic cures for social ills. At the same time it was claimed that the systems point of view was significant for its concern with causes rather than symptomatic problems. So went the swirl, until it became a circle devouring. Journalists present saw nothing concrete emerging from the circle and reported their frustration. Summary remarks at the close of the conference pointed to the move toward an interiority that characterizes the lives of increasing numbers of people and the evidence of such a move within the group present. This interiority was contrasted with the bold proposals for social action being proffered by many just a few years ago.

I was most interested, as a participant, in the intensity and emotion involved in refuting the position taken by the leader of the ashrams. This conflict showed the strong desire of the culture at large to refute the urge toward simpler, more contemplative, less frantic life styles. External fighting symbolizes a much more significant internal struggle. This internal battle, increasing in strength, is food for my Phoenix. The simplification involved in ashram-like living seems to be an essential beginning for the conversions called for by the present crisis facing the planet. Genuinely new ways of seeing the world can emerge from such contexts, and, out of altered constructions of what is called real, the culture can be sufficiently transformed to allow life to flourish.

Such moves become a kind of stopping of the world as Don Juan expresses it, a stopping in order to see anew. Daniel Berrigan expresses the same notion in one of his lines: "Don't just do something, Buddha said, stand there." This standing shared in a community of persons wanting to so stand is my own brand of participation in the development of consciousness and cultural transformation. I find this time to be one of scaling down my dreams and ridding myself of expectations, especially those professional pressures to continue in a certain direction. Better than anyone, Eliot described the time in "East Coker" from his *Four Quartets*:

> I said to my soul, be still, and wait without hope
> For hope would be hope for the wrong thing; wait without love
> For love would be love of the wrong thing; there is yet faith
> But the faith and love and the hope are all in the waiting.
> Wait without thought, for you are not ready for thought:
> So the darkness shall be the light, and the stillness the dancing.

NOTES

1. Rosemary Haughton develops this argument well in her article, "Deschooling and Education," *Commonweal* 97, No. 16 (January 26, 1973), 367-71.

2. The problem of means and ends is crucial in any discussion of social change, especially in the personal search for how to act. Insufficient reflection on means-ends issues is at the heart of so many wasted efforts to change the schools.

3. Jacques Ellul's *The Political Illusion* (New York: Vintage Books, 1972) is a beautiful critique for the potential curriculum theory illusion. Simply substitute curriculum theory where he uses the word political.

4. This is his description of doubt, which he sees as pervading much of present existence. See Karl Barth, *Evangelical Theology* (New York: Holt, Rinehart and Winston, 1963).

5. Soren Kierkegaard, *The Sickness unto Death*, tr. Walter Lowrie (New York: Doubleday Anchor Books, 1954), p. 162.

6. *Ibid.*, p. 175.

7. *Ibid.*, p. 147.

8. Rieff's book, *The Triumph of the Therapeutic*, Harper Torchbook (New York: Harper and Row, 1968), is a must for understanding the therapy part of current consciousness development.

9. Michael Polanyi exposes the objectivist dilemma with much clarity in his *Personal Knowledge*, Harper Torchbook (New York: Harper and Row, 1964), esp. chs. 7 and 8.

10. Richard J. Pilder analyzes this tendency of the encounter group to create its own myth while demythologizing much of the prevailing culture in a paper: "Encounter: A Demythologizing Myth Maker" (available from author).

11. Erich Newmann, *Art and the Creative Unconscious*, Bollinger Paperback (Princeton, New Jersey: Princeton University Press, 1971), p. 163.

12. Gwyneth Cravens interviewed Castaneda for *Harper's Magazine* 246, No. 1473 (February 1973), 91. Her article is entitled, "Talking to Power and Spinning with the Ally."

13. John C. Lilly, *Center of the Cyclone* (New York: Julian Press, 1972).

14. The notion of a political economy of images is created by Denis Goulet and offers a profoundly fruitful perspective on contemporary consciousness development.

15. Reported in Morton A. Lieberman, Irving D. Yalom, and Matthew B. Miles, "Encounter: The Leader Makes a Difference," *Psychology Today* 6, No. 10 (March 1973), 69-76.

16. See Paul Tillich's formulation of faith in his *The Courage to Be*, Harper Torchbook (New York: Harper and Row, 1958).

17. Donella H. Meadows, Dennis L. Meadows, Jorgen Randers, William W. Behrens III, *The Limits to Growth* (New York: New American Library, Signet, 1972).

18. Theodore Roszak, *Where the Wasteland Ends* (New York: Doubleday, 1972).

REACTIONS

A. AN ALL-AMERICAN SMALL GROUP IN SEARCH OF AN ELECTRIC KOOL-AID ACID THEORY OF CURRICULUM, OR, A HIGH IS NOT FOR HOME

Robert L. Osborn

Any resemblance between the following account of the life of a small group at a curriculum conference dealing with higher consciousness and an account that any other member of the group might write is problematic, to say the most for it. On the other hand, higher consciousness acknowledges the possibility of a multitude, if not an infinitude, of realities, and from this it follows that another reality is always worthy of investigation for whatever meaning it may possess. What follows was not written to belittle the experience of the group. Indeed, as small groups often go in a conference context, this one was eminently successful, that is to say, it developed a life and consciousness of its own, which added meaning to the overall conference experience for each participant. And this is a report on the content of that life and consciousness as it developed through the course of the conference.

At the first group meeting, immediately following Robert Starratt's presentation, a dozen or so strangers assembled and stared at each other across the gulfs that separate strangers. Each wore whatever face he had brought for the occasion, some with more confidence than others. From behind these faces they searched tentatively for each other. One or two knew each other at least by name; the remainder were known only by information gleaned from a conference name tag. Three questions seemed to stand out in the word exchanges as the group gathered and sought direction: Who are you? Why are we assembled here? What is this conference all about? Little beyond the questions had been formulated.

While this might seem an inauspicious beginning, that did not prove to be the case. The people who gathered for the first meeting returned for subsequent meetings and usually remained much longer than the time alloted. Their number grew substantially during the course of the conference, and rarely were they reduced to playing the game of "Small Group at a Curriculum Conference." Indeed, the group developed an integrity of its own. It functioned over the course of the conference to create and serve its own dynamics in a way that was significantly independent of, although clearly related to, the main sessions of the conference. By the second or third group session, somewhat disparate bits and pieces had become themes. They appeared and reappeared in various guises, and, with each return, took on a heightened sense of concern, if not urgency. Some of the bits were questions, and some were answers. The stimulus came from the conference papers, each of which sounded in its own way a call for recognition of "higher consciousness." While the papers were uniformly good and four were superb, they also became a source of profound disquietude. Higher consciousness does not make a comfortable home for most Americans, even those at a conference where higher consciousness represents the main theme. Each paper confronted the members of this small group with songs of mystery and revolution, songs that, however winsome or compelling, led down paths uncharted to worlds largely unknown. For safety's sake, men in such situations often return home, and so, it seemed, did the members of this group. They needed a place where they could find respite, where they could ask questions and seek answers drawn from their own consciousness in order, perhaps, to protect that consciousness. There is probably no better place to do that than home, and, if home is far away, then perhaps one can be found or created on the spot.

The conference was a high. This was only partly because of the superior quality of some of the papers. More particularly, it grew out of the special content of the papers. These originated in or dealt with esoteric experiences and perceptions of a counterculture steeped in mystery and revolution and pointing toward the unknown. Starratt could be dealt with, for he only urged humanity in the name of survival. Huebner moved us rather gently from humanity to higher consciousness. Pinar took us on a Jung and acid trip into the "inner or transcendental self," suggesting that, if we did not come along, we remained to murder ourselves. Bateman, telling it like it is, equated the higher consciousness with revolution and confronted us with the proposition that establishment curriculums, some even masked in the rhetoric of higher consciousness, oppress and thus murder the spirit. Greene, in a way putting Pinar and Bateman together, urged us to liberate our students through a process of self-reflection leading to authenticity and thence to action against powerlessness. For her, the full act of liberation led from what is to what should be. Macdonald tuned in on the transcendental and tantalized us with a technologized world of harmonious vibrations and children levitating in front of the TV. At this point curriculum looked at from the perspective of a "higher consciousness" was both heavy and heady, and, whatever other problems remained unresolved, both curriculum and school could conceivably foster the requisite consciousness. Pilder stopped that nonsense. He asserted flatly that the higher consciousness stood outside school and curriculum and that no amount of tinkering with either could bring it into being. The "new politics" could only grow out of an inner power derived from new selves generated through new relationships characterized by conviviality. The small groups did not meet after Pilder's paper, but they had been wrestling with the ghost of his message during much of the conference. Yes, the conference was a high. It excited the participants with showers of images of the delights and dreams inherent in the exploration of higher consciousness, but it also raised commensurate specters of fear and guilt. The guilt originated in the tension between blandishments concerning higher consciousness and doubts about one's ability as a person or a teacher to live comfortably with that consciousness. For some, there was even the nagging thought that we should not go there, that higher consciousness represented evil rather than good, an evil that was all too tempting. The fear, however, only partially grew out of fear of the unknown. It was also nurtured by a suspicion that the pursuit of higher consciousness meant the end of teachers, schools, and curriculums as now constituted, and maybe even the end of curriculum theory. Pilder, in the words and manner of a gentle prophet, said just that.

In contrast to the general sessions, where the theorists set forth their ideas, the small group became a home to its members. In that setting, names were attached to faces, and faces gained personalities and points of view. Early in the conference, therefore, its members got beyond the question, "Who are you?" They seemed to find out all they needed to know, and for the most part they seemed to like, or at least be content with, what they found out about each other. They discovered that they held more in common with each other than they shared with the authors of the papers delivered upstairs.

While no explicit consensus developed to answer the question, "Why are we assembled here?" still the behavior of the group did in a way answer that question, too. In the general sessions of the conference, members of the group underwent an intense intellectual and emotional experience at the hands of the theorists. While one must be careful not to overextend a metaphor, the group provided a place in which to come down. It was a place where one could ask troubling questions and get more comfortable answers. It was a place where the listener could deal with the material presented in terms more amenable to his own frame of reference and less threatening to his own personal and professional existence. He had to let himself down from the intensity of the experience; he had to begin dealing with the "higher consciousness" message sometime; he had to get back to a more familiar world. The group provided a place where this could occur, "with a little help from one's friends."

That home and higher consciousness did not rest too easily together became clear early in the conference, and it became even clearer as the conference proceeded. After learning each other's names, and after the leader of the group had proposed that its purpose was to discover a way of contributing more substantially to the proceedings of the conference, someone asked what the conference was all about. A touch of sharpness in the questioner's voice conveyed somewhat more meaning than the words spoken. During the course of the conference this question returned in a number of different guises, though not always from the same source. Regardless of the source, however, the question seemed implicitly to suggest that this curriculum theory conference had been taken over by heretics. Certainly it was not like curriculum theory conferences back home. In the first place it was too philosophical, and, if not that, certainly the poets and philosophers of higher consciousness sang very different songs from those the group was used to. Higher consciousness fare seemed to make strange philosophical grounding for curriculum theory. Where were the usual philosophical grounds for curriculum, like democracy or the eternal verities? Where were the more familiar questions and issues? Had the child been tossed out of the curriculum? Should not there have been a paper on an "Inquiry-Centered Curriculum?" Was Bruner, along with structure, dead?

While it is very exciting to speculate about the possibilities of developing higher consciousness through the curriculum, the teachers and curriculum specialists in this small group kept returning to the practical. In a word, back home awaited pupils to teach and teachers to prepare, and the higher speculations contained in the conference papers neglected such everyday realities. For the most part, no one spelled out what would happen to history or algebra in a curriculum designed to nourish higher consciousness, or what a schedule of classes might look like, or even whether a schedule of classes would be required. Similarly, what would a methods class do differently if it were attempting to prepare teachers to foster higher consciousness? Would a methods seminar still talk about classroom control, or would the very idea of control be antithetical to the nurture of higher consciousness? If there was one concept that this small group was at home with—only one member of the group dissenting—it was with the belief that schooling and social life in general required ultimate control of and responsibility for the behavior of children, which must reside in the hands of proper authorities such as parents and teachers. While the papers had not denied the need for some level or order of control, they had for the most part left this issue open. By implication, moreover, they had challenged conventional beliefs about control. The small group remained committed to control, and, while this commitment surfaced in relation to practical problems, the difference ran deeper than this. What seemed to be at stake were basic beliefs about the nature of man.and the conditions required for civilized living; but concern for the practical captured the attention of the group. Admittedly, the advertised subject of the conference was curriculum theory, and, while that has a place, those back home claim to prefer the practical to the theoretical.

This sums up the reaction of one group to curriculums of higher consciousness. From the outside it may seem an unduly superficial reaction, perhaps more emotive than cerebral, more stream of consciousness than philosophical, more talk than discourse. Clearly the group did not respond to the theories presented in a thoroughly critical and systematic way. For the most part, it failed to grapple with the basic issues, which suggests that the members of the group may have missed much of the point of the conference and much of the message of the individual presentations. Moreover, the group tended to treat them as if they represented identical points of view. In failing to distinguish substantial differences among them, crucial issues involving these differences were neglected.

Still, the particular reaction of the group does point to a fundamental problem facing exponents of curriculums of higher consciousness, Pilder being only somewhat the exception. In effect, the members of this group served notice that curriculums of higher consciousness did not fit agreeably into their own consciousness of curriculum.
In spite of the enchantment of the message conveyed at the conference, members of the group heard that message from across a formi-
dable ideological gulf, a gulf that would widen as each member of the
group returned to his "home" high school or college. In similar vein,
a concern for the "practical" grew at least to some extent from the
focus on theory, but it also developed out of recognition by the
group that theoretical differences frequently signal differences over
matters of practice or of what is practical. Every member of the
group had very likely experienced occasions when moves to liberalize
curriculum had been defeated on the grounds that such a step would
not be practical at the time. In this context, "not practical" suggests,
among other things, that a given move, however theoretically attractive, would not be implemented because of the negative climate
existing among faculty and community.

Thus, while the speakers posed profound theoretical and practical
problems for the group, the group in turn represented and symbolized very real problems for the curricular theorists. However en-
chanted the group was with the idea of a curriculum of higher consciousness, it remained only an enchantment. Not one member of the
group gave evidence of returning home a convert prepared to work
for suggested curricular reforms. However high a member of the
group had become during the conference, he realized in franker moments that he had not moved beyond exhilaration and some heady
knowledge. He would return home substantially the person that de-
parted. He realized that if he stood this far from the positions of
Pinar and Pilder, then those back home stood even farther removed.
How could anyone realistically propose a curriculum of higher consciousness for American schools and expect that it would be implemented? While the theorists did to some extent address this question,
it still represents and symbolizes the challenge they face in society at
large. Having failed to convince the microcosm, how can they hope
to convince the macrocosm? Or, which comes first, the microcosm or
the macrocosm?

With the close of the conference, the small group broke up. As it did so, its members, no longer strangers, touched each other, shook hands, or waved good-bye. Without exception, each still basked somewhat in the high the conference had generated, and their voices conveyed this as they agreed that it had been a great conference. With that, each left the hotel and prepared for the long ride home.

B. REACTIONS OF A GROUP LEADER

Charles W. Beegle

Curriculum workers seem to be caught in a maze of logistical concerns—organization for learning, developing learning packages, and rearranging school artifacts of yesteryear. New forms and new language must be devised for shaping curriculum in order to avoid logistical dead ends. It would appear to be imperative that curriculum workers clarify goals or intentions before concentrating on logistical designs. Pinar, Starratt, Huebner, Bateman, Macdonald, Greene, and Pilder, along with the discussion groups, have provided input for rearranging thought patterns and for raising more important questions than those that we often pursue. Key questions in curriculum planning grew out of group discussions: What kinds of human beings do educators hope the young can become or just be? What kinds of experience provide for openness in human beings? Must we treat the system as a given? Does societal growth or improvement come about through reform in education or political action? Can we have a viable educational institution in an absurd society?

As man's horizon expands through technology, moon and space exploration, atomic energy, computers, and unprecedented expansions of knowledge, man needs to find ways to make use of this knowledge so that he does not become a slave to his own inventions. Man has been so concerned about scientific rationality, as our scientific-industrial society has developed during the last five centuries, that its center rests more and more outside the human personality. An understanding of technology alone cannot develop the whole man, however. Macdonald's concern for aesthetic rationality points toward an alternative to solve problems and reflect upon man's environment. Aesthetics, as I understand Macdonald's use of the term, means man's capacity to deal rationally with the world on an intuitive basis. He urges that man return to the world of insights, which can lead him beyond the present system of thought, to carry on dialogue "between the individual and his environment" and also between the individual and his self. This growing consciousness has always resided in the minds of men, but it has been avoided in discussions of knowledge and education.

The view that the environment of civilized mankind is insulted by willful stupidity echoed throughout a number of the presentations. It appears that man has taken a dangerous tool (new knowledge and cybernetics) by the blade instead of the handle. Civilization could destroy its own chances if these new tools further impinge on the space in which man finds himself. Contemporary problems of a pluralistic society—racial, religious, political, socioeconomic, ecological, psychological, often giving rise to hostility or even overt conflict—cannot be solved in the present context of our societal institutions. An ontological shift from outer life to inner life must be encouraged.

Ross Mooney's conceptual life system model (taken from *Evaluation in Higher Education: Ground, Goal, and Way to Go* [Lansing, Michigan: Michigan Association of Colleges and Universities, 1967], Figure 1) provides a meaningful framework to bring order out of the numerous points of view presented at this conference. In such a model the organism must be open to its environment and integrative in its being; it must participate in a transactional give and take of energies across its borders and selectively form fresh fittings in creative transformations as time passes.

Openness refers to an individual's receptivity to the stimuli about him, to the sights, sounds, touches, smells, tastes, events, and ideas that impinge on him. Developing an understanding of one's relationship with his environment seems imperative. Another common thread that seems to run throughout a number of the major presentations is the idea of centering the person in the world, integrating the human organism in his environment. How do we bring elements into a whole that would permit the human organism to move in a variety of ways, integrating and transforming?

Macdonald raises questions that relate very well to the life systems model: What kinds of activity are encouraged that provide for opening perceptual experiences? What kinds of activity facilitate the process of sensitizing people to others and to inner vibrations? What kinds of activity provide experiences for developing close-knit community relationships? What kinds of activity encourage and facilitate religious experience? What kinds of activity facilitate the develop-

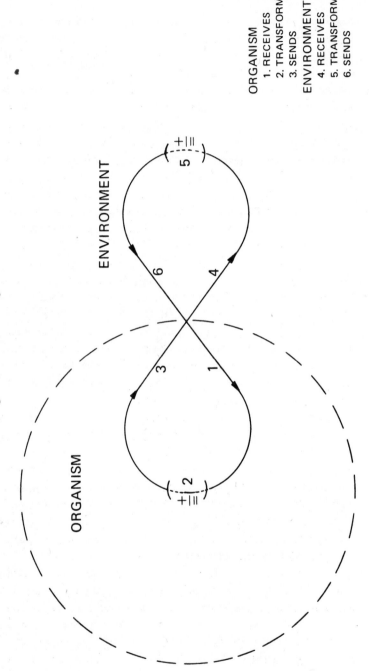

Figure B-1. Model of a life system, an organism, open and integrative, in continuous give and take with the environment, effecting transformations through selective fittings

ENVIRONMENT

ORGANISM

ORGANISM
1. RECEIVES
2. TRANSFORMS
3. SENDS
ENVIRONMENT
4. RECEIVES
5. TRANSFORMS
6. SENDS

ment of patterned meaning structures? What ways can we organize knowledge to enlarge human potential through meaning? How can we facilitate the development of inner strength and power in human beings?

Pinar's development of the "inner-outer orientation as an explicative device for understanding the crucial distinction between the dominant culture and the counterculture"; Greene's suggestion that curriculum be conceived as a source of "reciprocity of perspectives" upon man's own perspectives, the awakening to pursue clarity for self-consciousness; Pilder's "struggle to integrate the profound personal experience of inner power and subsequent cultural transformations—all reiterate what Mooney expresses through his conceptual design. This conceptual framework provides promise for students who have been struggling with curricular concerns at this conference.

Openness to experience is limited to those events or stimuli of the external world that seem to the individual to relate to the inner life. More significant than receptivity to the external world is man's openness with respect to his own inner life. He has fewer internal barriers, that is, experience; he is self-accepting.

The conference suggests that, in developing curriculum experiences, one should work toward altering defenses that psychologically cripple students. Educators need to develop growth-fostering experiences that will encourage openness, trust, and security rather than hostility, distrust, and insecurity, which thicken and harden the perceptive screen. Becoming more aware of perceptions is a beginning; the individual must look inward to gain direction for continued development.

Curriculum development should also reflect that human existence and living things in general have being only as they maintain themselves in an environmental setting. Living organisms must continually give and take within their setting. In essence, as Mooney suggests, this is a regenerating, renewing existence. As man interacts with his environment, he changes it. As man changes his environment, it in turn changes his behavior. Life, therefore, is creative by its very nature, fitting to a world that is in continuous change.

The individual is not powerless in his setting. Bateman's comment seems appropriate: "It is our task, each one of us, to come to grips with what is known, to take a stand, to decide whether to be a part of the problems or a part of the solutions." And this is exactly where

Pilder finds himself: "To be specific, I no longer can hope to relate curriculum theory to the major upheavals occurring in persons at the level where culture resides. Culture is not out there somewhere; culture is where we live, the place of our indwelling. This mutuality is precisely what is absent in the places at work now available. . . . The time is now to begin living the changes, and dialogue needs to occur about this living."

Pilder is saying, I believe, that it is time to stop, to develop a heightened awareness, seeking genuinely new ways of seeing the world—developing introspection busy with innerness or outerness, not just acting from habit or as a slave to societal pressures and expectations. He is reiterating what M. C. Richards (*Centering* [Middletown, Connecticut: Wesleyan University Press, 1969], p. 7) expresses: "This is the main thing. This is what I care about, it is the person. This is the living vessel: person. This is what matters. This is our universe. This is the task, the joy and dolor: to be born as person, to live and love as person; to dwell in the world as in a person. The living spirit, the moving form, the living word, life-death, art-life, corpus, body, being, all, persons. Truly life is absent in the moment when person is eliminated. This is the urgency of my speech—for this occasion and all human occasions—to bring man into man's consciousness."

C. SOME REACTIONS

William T. Lowe

You are hereby warned that this is not good reporting. My preju-
dices heavily color my reactions to the conference. This is true in
part because my discussion group never really functioned as intended. The membership changed, and we frequently failed to discuss the scheduled topic. Further, we did not stay together and
sometimes had as many as three subgroups operating. Even those
hardy souls who attended every session might not recognize the reactions that follow. For a variety of reasons, however, I am not concerned about my failure as a reporter. The major function of these
responses should be to provide some additional perspectives, or, to
use a cliché of our times, to provide alternatives, not group consensus.

"What's a nice guy like Starratt doing at a crazy conference like
this?" I do not know who said this, but I did hear it, and I agree that
his message did not fit. Father Starratt is a leftish-leaning centrist, a
classically educated Roman Catholic intellectual—*Commonweal*, all
the way. He is articulate, urbane, witty, charming, handsome, and
straight. Playing the role to the hilt, he accurately summarizes some
of the persistent points of controversy among curriculum theorists
and predictably urges the middle or comfortably left-of-the-exact-
center course. He also pleads for more study of and emphasis on
world order, peace, justice, human dignity, and so on. In two of the
three major sections of his presentation, he is saying what has seldom
been said in any more pleasing way, but it has been said many times
before.

For some discussants, Starratt's grouping of scholars is unfortunate. It is a broad category, indeed, that makes ideological bedfel-
lows of Broudy, Stanley, Hutchins, Rickover, and Barr, all of whom
are assigned to the "citizenship" group. Starratt may not be entirely

fair to some authors, either, perhaps because he connects his remarks to so many authorities. In one such instance he charges Silberman with a middle-class bias because of his praise for suburban schools when, in fact, positive as well as negative examples in Silberman's work come from communities of various socioeconomic levels.

Good things for Starratt include: striking a balance, a healthy balance, "mixing it up" in the political arenas, acting responsibly, and reform. Bad things are composed in part of deschooling, quoting Marcuse, Roszak, and Reich without action, abolition of authority, power, and law, and exclusive concentration on anything.

His attack on an argument of Joseph Schwab is less familiar. Starratt wants the people who were invited to this conference (mostly "college types" from education faculties) to become philosophers. He wants us to avoid history of philosophy, ordinary language or linguistic analysis, and "meticulous commentaries on previous philosophers," and he pleads for a "vigorous revival of philosophical inquiry." He hopes that we will produce a currently recognized Dewey, Mill, James, Whitehead, and so on. The group talked about such things as: Does any generation appropriately recognize its philosophers? Does our age truly lack them? Is it possible that one or more of our significant contemporary philosophers attended this conference? How would you recognize one in print or in person? Certain writers have been quoted again and again in these papers. Why do they not qualify?

The group then moved to Starratt's position that it is neither possible nor desirable to become the multipurposed educator, the philosopher-practitioner, all rolled into one. There were grave doubts. This separation seemed dangerous. It was felt that harried practitioners should get more than some stimulation from Toffler; some might even make some changes based on their own study, without using a middle man.

Other similar questions were raised, and still more interesting items occurred to me later. Starratt is correct. This piece by Schwab deserves more reflection than it has received, and we are indebted to Starratt for pointing the way.

Starratt really did what was asked of him: he outlined the "state of the field of curriculum theory." That most of it was predictable and rather trite probably says more about the field than about the paper.

Starratt was apparently the only consultant given any degree of specificity in his assignment. Dwayne Huebner, like the others, was simply asked to develop a broad theme. This being the case, it is interesting that Huebner begins by apologizing—saying that his presentation is probably the wrong subject for the wrong audience at the wrong time. It would be fascinating to know what he thought would have been the right subject for this audience at this time. In any event, consistent with his apology, he uses this opportunity to continue his long-term effort toward clarification of the concepts or language of curriculum. Only indirectly does he address himself to the stated theme.

Perhaps the closest connection to the theme is the suggestion that hermeneutics may provide a synthesizing tool for relating the cultural revolution and the desire for heightened consciousness to curriculum development. Clearly, the notion of exegetic interpretation can be used in seeking an understanding of inner as well as outer phenomena. Even the potentially useful notion of hermeneutics, however, seems to belong more to instruction than to curriculum theory. Actually, I am not at all certain what Huebner means by curriculum. (Indeed, upon reflection and becoming entirely personal, hermeneutics, by that name, may well have had a profound influence in the development of my own frame of reference or way of patterning. I grew up surrounded by seminarians, where the older youth were role models. Their enthusiastic but serious "you wouldn't understand" talk of hermeneutics class intrigued me. I pleaded to hear examples of classroom exercises. I do not recall having heard the word since then.)

The essay contains some interesting and helpful suggestions about the murky language of the field. For example, the distinction between learning, schooling, and education is beautifully drawn. The reflexive nature of our language and our ways of thinking is clarified. The separation of educational issues from efficiency or narrow economic questions is stimulating.

There is a surprising conservatism, given Huebner's reputation for avant-gardism. He seems firmly rooted in a tripartite individual, society, culture tradition that stems from Tyler's model. Further, the world of the middle-class intellectual with books, electric typewriters, and parents who read to their children is portrayed as ideal.

I rely on my own judgment in supporting Huebner's opening

comment: this probably is the wrong subject for the wrong audience at the wrong time, but it is an interesting effort.

There was little discussion of Pinar's work. Time was short, and our understanding of the author's message was limited. Since Pinar also planned the conference, his presentation exhibits a consistency of purpose lacking in most of the other efforts, and it provides the best introduction to this volume. I believe that the group should have stayed with its provocative content until each member had some operational definition for each major aspect of the theme: heightened consciousness, cultural revolution, and curriculum theory. This is not to suggest that Pinar provided *the* meanings of the three, but he did stimulate me, at least, to search for answers; further, his explication provided some kind of unity for all of the presentations.

In my view, Pinar played an interesting and potentially presumptuous role in his statement. Clearly he was one of the group: his academic credentials are entirely in order; he holds a professorship; he planned a conference with a series of lectures and without an encounter group orientation; he even received a typical challenge from a radical member of the audience. He is, however, very young, and his remarks suggest that he knows his way around in the counterculture. In fact, there is an autobiographical flavor to much of his description of inner-directedness. He warns the audience that they do not know much about the topic, thereby creating a fairly deliberate personification of the bridge in the generation gap. More than that, he boldly hints that he has a foot in both the dominant culture and the counterculture. Even more, the speaker lumped those gathered, with few exceptions, as representative of the dominant culture. The man has courage!

Let me raise some of the questions that occur to me as I examine Pinar's study. First, his notion of curriculum is not clear to me. He seems to include classroom interactions, teaching strategies and approaches, subject matter, narrowly conceived goals, and broad philosophical orientations. It would be helpful to know more specifically what he means. Since the entire effort involves curriculum theory building, this should be important.

But, what is probably even more significant, how valid is it to suggest that the counterculture, meaning the drive for understanding self and developing heightened consciousness as well as a rebelliousness against conventional norms, is either more prevalent than at other times, or more likely to have an impact on the mainstream society, or more durable? I regret to say that I perceive the evidence to point unmistakably toward neither intense inner (psychological)- or outer (sociopolitical)-directedness but rather toward apathy, conformity, and a lack of concern. While I hope Pinar is right, I fear that the "distinguishable hiatus" argument is largely a myth. Even the volume of literature about the subject is not uniquely heavy in our times. I simply do not believe that cultural revolution is around the next corner, alas.

There are many other less-important questions. For example, I doubt that the only way, or even the best way, to know about counterculturism is to be a part of it. Further, "getting high" is not exclusively a need of counterculturists. Music, art, drinking, theater, exotic foods, and other recreational and re-creating functions serve for many of us. Then, too, given the premises of the counter-culture, can or should anyone else try to devise a curriculum to serve them, or must they devise their own? (Pilder makes this point so well.)

But enough quibbling; there is raw explanatory power in this essay. The outline of the history of "the movement" is valuable. The explanation of the potential roles of drugs, Eastern thought, and the "return to nature" is useful. There is an issue of tremendous, even staggering significance here: should the school or can the school be deliberately or primarily engaged in helping people recognize, explore, and disclose their inner selves? Even if the cultural revolution is not as widespread as Pinar seems to believe, such a goal assumes prime significance. Even if the young were not still involved in this movement, which is clearly not the case, the school should lead toward this end if Pinar is right. The implications are enormous. Every aspect of the school—its governance, organization, curriculum, instruction—would need to be changed. As I said, he has courage and also, I believe, rare insight.

Bateman joins Bruner, Oliver, and others active in the curriculum development movement of the 1960's in claiming that those developers made a tragic mistake. He lambastes the national projects of the period and strongly criticizes the "Romantic School Critics." While humanistic education has more appeal for Bateman than the academic recommendations of the period, it does not constitute a solution, either. In fact, in this passionate paper Bateman strikes out at reformers of every ilk. He insists that our culture is so laden with racism, sexism, classism, materialism, and violence that reform just will not work; revolution is required. Further, the school, like all of our contemporary institutions, is evil, and school people use every possible device, subtle and blatant, to maintain the status quo with continued domination by the school elite.

We are told that the school is political, like it or not, and that neutrality is quite impossible. One supposes, although Bateman does not actually say so, that the school must be actively political. It must take sides. It must lead to the good society. I was reminded of George Counts and Theodore Brameld and the social reconstruction movement, although Bateman never mentions this tradition.

If this kind of political leadership from schools is what Bateman really wants, then there appears to be a marked conflict with the inner, psychological thrust suggested by other authors in this series. When challenged with this observation in the discussion group, however, Bateman denied any contradiction. This denial left the group somewhat confused as to Bateman's view of needed curriculum theory or directions. Nothing seemed above attack, but no viable substitutes were suggested. Jenck's notion of a school that is more pleasant for students, parents, and teachers was softly praised, and, at the same time, nonabrasive conformity was bitterly attacked. I am not certain what Professor Bateman wants, but the severity of his criticism requires that it lead somewhere.

Maxine Greene is a wordsmith, and her work has a poetic quality. The vocabulary, rhetoric, and syntax are both attractive and complex, which leads one to question what she really is saying. Her beautiful piece of work was hard to pin down. There was so much room for movement, for shades of interpretation.

Schools, she feels, are oppressive and mechanistic, but "awakening" can occur in them and so they should remain. The disciplines should be taught, but it is individual perspectives and patterns that are of most worth. We must try to create a humanizing curriculum within a kind of fixed social reality that includes behavioral objectives and other evils; yet, "our obligation as educators is to enable students to take action against such powerlessness." "Learning is significant only when it responds to personal necessity," but "it is trivial to focus primarily on affect and sensitivity." We read the phrase "*mere* innerness or introspection," yet inner space and time and awareness seem to be at the heart of her view of curriculum. I am humbled by this experience and its imagery, and I lack understanding; I must read it again.

This is a very clear-cut statement of an ideological position, and Macdonald contrasts it to four additional ideologies, showing the faults of the others and the strengths of his own transcendental developmental theory. Like it or not, there it is. He also describes the foundations of his structure, drawing objectively, I believe, on James, Jung, and Polanyi, among others, but particularly on the centering notion of Mary Caroline Richards. In quite explicit terms he discusses potential implications and consequences of his position by providing specific goals, pedagogical processes, roles of disciplines, teachers, and students. It is all there in tightly reasoned prose—the kind of paper I wish I could write.

I also wish there had been more attention to the differences between his position and that of the Romantic ideologists; more detail about what to do when the inevitably conflicting expectations of various participants in the learning process collide; more information on protecting the transcending developing learner from the harsh demands of social realities. For example, some children, and also some parents and some teachers, not even to mention more removed individuals, do not want learners to transcend. They want to be told how to "make it" right now in our grubby materialistic world. What then, Mr. Macdonald? Most of all, however, because of the considerable accomplishments of this paper, I would like to hear more from this man—much more.

Pilder's quick, accurate, and generally supportive overviews end with the observation that much of significance has been said here about potential philosophies of life, but little about the realities of curriculum building. He goes on to explain this. You must, however, experience his thoughts for yourself. They draw forth a reverence and an awe, an atmosphere where one can feel the eloquence, the truth, and the agony. Pilder's professional despair becomes an intensely personal thing for many of us. And I lack his Phoenix.

Instead of searching, I tried to escape; I drove to the suburbs and mowed the lawn—no stillness, no dancing, no tightrope walking for me.

D. REACTIONS TO THE CONFERENCE: AN INTERPRETATION

George Willis

> If one is lucky, he finds that life does not fit into theoretical frames
> .... Kierkegaard insisted, and I agree with him, that a logical system
> is possible but that an existential system is not .... Exploration of
> the interior life begins properly with memories and themes.
> —Ralph Harper, *The Existential Experience*

If the modern gods of the curriculum theorist are dead, they died
before this conference began. What killed them was doubtless the
growing professional awareness that the solution to curricular problems cannot be reached through the usual liturgies of theoretical
constructs, behavioral objectives, structures of the disciplines, or factor analysis. The conference did not kill them, but it did take their
deaths seriously. In one form or another each of the presentations
dwelt on themes arising from their deaths, and Pilder's directly articulated the immediate, disturbing consequences of this passing. The
conference participants lived with the consequences.

This is a hopeful sign but not an easy one. One does not rest easy
with the loss of faith in logical systems to solve curricular problems,
nor with the dreadful realization that after all there may be no
solutions. But it is hopeful to know that in loss and dread there is
still the beginning of meaning, that meaning can and must be made
anew by each person alone, and that this process begins deep in the
exploration of the themes of one's own interior experience. And it is
important for the curriculum theorist to remember this, for he would
help others make meaning. It is particularly hopeful, then, that the
conference invited participation in this process. We can at least hope,
therefore, that the conference might indicate some wide-scale deep-
ening of vision of those working in curriculum.

Two interrelated themes that emerged throughout the conference
deserve special mention, for they helped create the context of uneasi-
ness within which the discussions moved: the first dealt mainly with

outer experience and political reality; the second, with inner experience and personal meaning. Both, however, implied the same things, for both became reminders of professional, if not human, limitation.

The first theme concerns the oppression of pedagogy. Any pedagogy, however well intentioned, tends to become oppressive in itself, inevitably promoting that which it is intended to destroy. Each individual must demythologize his own world and take his own political action. Neither task can be done for him, and attempts to aid him may create new mythologies and hence new oppressions as quickly as they destroy the old. Are consciousness raising and cultural revolution compatible with curriculum in any form? This remains to be seen.

The second theme concerns interior experience. Put simply, interior experience cannot be systematized. No logical system can account for the ways in which the inner person remakes himself, providing personal meaning to his personal, inner world. How, then, can any curriculum be other than alien to this process, an unwanted logical intrusion into a process that shapes itself apart from sheer logical form? Again, this question remains unanswered.

Perhaps these themes of limitation and the foregoing analogy account at least in part for the character of the discussions in Group H. If heightened awareness of the limits of logical systems can bring the curriculum theorist to the void, it may also bring him to think existentially. Among the participants in these discussions, there seemed to be considerable initial awareness of professional limitations, then tentative identification of the character of this situation, and, finally, exploration of personal, interior themes that may have marked the beginning of increased professional meaning.

But like all basic existential recognitions, this process in itself is disquieting. Doubtless, not all engaged in it; nor did it necessarily occur in any particular sequence. In general, discussions were varied and sometimes disjointed. Seldom did the group respond to a presented paper as a whole or to its principal lines of argumentation. More often a paper provided some ideas, some fragments. These were constantly juxtaposed, rearranged, and viewed from multiple perspectives. The effect was quite kaleidoscopic: a series of interrelated images merging into one another without clearly discernible beginnings or ends. Fortunately, we reached few resolutions. And within this flux, however hazily or haltingly, some images and themes in part our own may have taken shape. What was suggested to us and what we suggested for ourselves is, of course, impossible to say. However, some recollection and arrangement of these fragments—now fragments of fragments—may indicate part of what outwardly occurred.

Following Starratt's presentation, the first discussion of Group H eventually came to touch on the nature of freedom. Comments began: Starratt seems not so much to be suggesting solutions to problems as to be suggesting a new image of man, and this image implies radical changes in the framework of schooling as we now know it. Is the school, therefore, becoming dysfunctional? No, it already is. Dysfunctionality is built into schools, for within them few people have an opportunity to exercise personal responsibility. What, then, about the potential dysfunctionality of theory itself or of any implementation that follows from it? Do not the uses of these ultimately tend to constrain the individual's responsibility and, therefore, to become incompatible with humane values? The problem is in part a political problem, but curriculum theory must develop a new way of viewing human freedom. Again, is this possible? Freedom may be a function of one's own purposes . . . . Thus the fragments tumbled.

After Huebner's presentation, we began again: Time is not a collection of discrete moments; we dwell in time. Teachers being present to students means being present temporally as well as physically, yet being present to one person involves many others. Problems arise due to confusion between language and reality, and confusion of this kind is destructive to the child. This confusion often takes the form of the discrepancy between the "free language" used to describe the schools and the "police structures" actually present in them. "Learning" seems omnipresent in the schools. Do we need, therefore, other descriptive paradigms besides "learning"? Teachers often feel guilty about talking "freedom" and doing, or being forced to do, "learning." . . .

Pinar's presentation produced further considerations: To what extent do schools create alienation? Schools do not seem to provide options that can relieve alienation. How much must the individual build his own curriculum, and how much can it be done for him? Frame of mind, attitude, and intentionality all seem important, but the individual must organize his own experiences. Predetermination of outcomes tends to delimit this possibility. To what extent, then, should a curriculum be devoted to consciousness raising? Can this in itself be sufficient? An important point may be that many young persons are already living with heightened consciousness. The schools need only to tap into it, and the curriculum can open up this process. The curriculum theorist, therefore, has considerable political responsibility for educating the public about what constitutes good educative experience, thereby aiding the process.

Bateman dealt with politics and outward experience, giving rise to our fourth session, which clearly centered on an extended discussion of the politics of change in the Rochester schools. Can change be created by demythologizing first, with no direct social action? That is, can it be done by recognition and identification of problems without direct efforts to change them? Again, the group reached no resolutions, only the suggestion that the ordinary process of change follows a sequence of demythologizing, consciousness raising, and political activity.

Following her presentation, Greene spoke jointly with Group H and Group I, illuminating our questions: How does one maintain contact with his background consciousness, become articulate about his biographical perceptions, make meanings? How can curriculum provide suggestions and possibilities that arouse amazement? Why does teaching involve risk and inevitable failure? Why does education inevitably involve suffering?

Macdonald's presentation preceded our final session, and also gave rise to questions: Was Macdonald himself "in transit" in his own thinking? Is "in transit" to be considered a negative or a positive state? Can and will his optimistic view of the humane uses of technology hold?

Once again, no resolutions. But then this comment: The deeper you go into curriculum theory, the more you realize you do not know; therefore, you deal with mystery. Yet mystery has long been a theme in theological and ontological thinking, and theologically it designates truth that surpasses human comprehension. We have moved far away from mystery since the Renaissance, with our emphasis on rationality and empiricism. Perhaps we can still make use of mystery. Then discussion ended.

Finally, Pilder described where we had been.

How many participants were lucky enough to have come having found beforehand where this might be, how many became aware, and how many returned unlucky and unaware cannot be known. Only intuitions remain. But this is as it should be. The best and worst that happens, happens inwardly, where memories begin and end and where our themes can merge. As Ralph Harper, the existential philosopher-theologian, put it:

Perhaps, after all, there is something that binds all . . . themes together, some feature of ourselves that appears first as contingency, turns threatening, and finally can be converted into a sense of the infinite. I would call it the state of being unfinished, for our experience, which is unfinished as long as we are alive, is always shifting and changing, being assaulted and assisted, refusing and being refused, welcoming and being welcomed. It is this vitality which justifies the image of the kaleidoscope. Everything is there, and we have a right to expect the unexpected (*The Existential Experience* [Baltimore: The Johns Hopkins University Press, 1972], p. 15).

E. THE LISTENERS

Francine Shuchat Shaw

Rather than attempt to formulate a critical restatement or comparative evaluation of the studies presented by the speakers at the Rochester Conference, I am more compelled to share my reflections on the other participants, the listeners. While I was able to feel both as one with the speakers as they articulately and passionately shared their thoughts and convictions, and as separate from them as I balanced their words with my own experiences, many other listeners found it difficult to maintain this state of being within and without. While I felt comfortable allowing time and space for the expression of ideologies that I might weigh against my own and assimilate with other convictions and understandings that I am in the process of forming, many others found listening in such a way problematic, found operating within a lecture-group discussion framework against their better judgment. As the listener's attention shifted from the essence of the presentations to this framework of the conference itself, so did the theme of the conference shift from "Heightened Consciousness, Cultural Revolution, and Curriculum Theory" to process, format, and methodology.

It is at once ironic and inevitable that a group of educators, being offered several varied and clear analyses of the problems of methodology they fight on their own homeground, would exhibit those same problems within their context at this conference. The odd brand of inoperability that characterized the listeners within this lecture-group discussion format bore a frightening resemblance to the learning problems of our own students. If we educators have had any part in creating the problems our students experience with the learning process, it may well be this very fact: we often refuse to take sufficient responsibility within a situation to make particular sorts of methodologies work for us at the expense of gaining from that which comes to us through those methodologies.

The Rochester Conference brought forth and exemplified for the listeners principles basic to, and problems inherent in, all things educational: the need to correlate content and methodology, to create a process for learning appropriate for that which is to be learned, and to develop a process that utilizes and exemplifies the very principles and concepts upon which the subject matter at hand is based. An instance of this might be an educator's decision to implement a workshop situation rather than a lecture format when teaching composition. The listeners translated these dilemmas at the Rochester Conference by identifying several kinds of disharmony between the content or nature of the speakers' papers and the format within which they were presented and discussed. If the papers were generally intended to be agents motivating dialogue and action with regard to the theoretical problems of curriculum and the relation of those problems to all things educational, societal and political, they were, perhaps, too successful; the listeners were so anxious to engage in dialogue, to actively participate in the generation of theory, that their apparent need was merely the existence of a conference without a planned program rather than one allowing time and space for external catalysts or stimuli through the ideologies of others. The listeners resented and rejected being talked at about engaging in educational activity within a lecture situation that rendered them immediately passive; hence, the paradox between the action- and activity-oriented essence of the papers and the seemingly disseminative nature of the methodology employed to convey them.

The listeners similarly responded to the suggested definition of the small group discussions that followed each speaker's presentation; while group members were asked to encourage clarification of and response to each paper among group members during these discussions, the listeners felt this kind of dialogue less useful and important than, again, active participation in the generation of theory. As a result, what actually happened in several of these small group discussions, and in the countergroup that met in lieu of attending the Friday afternoon presentation, points again to the problems educators have with their own learning process. Having decided not to give full attention or response to a group of speakers exploring personal, educational, societal, and political reasons and ways to achieve humanistic communication and growth for individuals and among groups, the listeners exhibited those very problems of defensiveness,

manipulation, and inflexibility that stand in the way of such human-
ism. The groups, for the most part, were not able to work as a
cohesive unit to accomplish their proposed effort, which was generation of theory and meaningful sharing of experience. Within the
groups I found preoccupations with definition, methodology, and
process pertaining to the groups themselves and with criticisms of the
format of the conference as a whole. I also found that one or several
persons emerged from a group as a leader, monopolizing the recount-
ing of experience or the dissemination of personal knowledge, a
situation vulnerable to the same criticism leveled at the larger conference by the listeners, themselves. Such behaviors render the listener's
frequent response to the presentations as "old stuff" meaningless.
They were incapable of dealing not only with the essence of the
presentations and the format of the conference but also with each
other, making obvious the listener's need to listen now and then, to
prepare themselves occasionally for external stimuli, to learn the
process of being within and without in order to permit assimilation
of new ideas and the cultivation of flexibility. Perhaps a preoccupation with the format and the definition of an experience inhibits
what one might gain from it; if so, this indicates a need for responsibility on the part of the listeners. On the other hand, particular
methodologies might inhibit and impair learning in an absolute sense
and, therefore, demand total rejection in all situations. One should
decide, upon receiving notice and description of such a conference,
whether to attend and operate within its definition and format, to
attend and stir the waves from within because of inoperability, or
simply not to attend at all.

The general discrepancy between content and method and the
specific question of the validity of lecturing at the potential expense
of learning through doing are problems we all encounter as we
assume the roles of decision makers. It is for this reason, and because
I want to affirm our need to identify and make an issue of such a
discrepancy, that I stress this theme here. Methods derived from the
theoretical concepts of discovery, student-centeredness, and teacher
indirection, if you will permit this oversimplification, are often at
odds with the lecture format, often to the point of totally excluding
it. While I am a humanist in both theory and practice and attempt to
encourage high degrees of activity for my own students and fellow
learners, I think it unrealistic and unfortunate to write off the lecture

format for particular purposes and occasions. We and our students know not how to involve ourselves with lecture or take proper responsibility for it in order to allow the realization of its virtues at appropriate times. The extent to which we can and should employ a methodology that exemplifies the principles of a specific subject matter is a complex problem and largely a matter of individual capability, practicality, and receptivity. As I have implied throughout this essay, it seems to me that we should allow time and space for expressions of individual ideology, a form of external stimuli that can often come to us through the lecture-group discussion format, with which we can then interact and, perhaps, reformulate. Given this opportunity, the responsibility is on the listeners.

Other conference circles have anticipated these discrepancies and tried to avoid them. The title of the August meeting of the National Council of Teachers of English in Kalamazoo is "the unconference." It is to be "characterized by informality, openness and vitality":

—with no rigid theme to follow and no stiff statement of purpose
—with workshops of not more than 20 people, where the emphasis will be on dialogue, not lecture
—with scheduled meetings only as indicated by interest—no meetings for meeting's sake
—with a no-holds-barred approach to controversial issues, real problems of the profession, gripes . . . and with plenty of open mikes so your voices can be heard.

I do not draw from the literature of the NCTE "unconference," or from its directors' important efforts, in order to criticize the Rochester Conference by comparison. Nor, I might add, have I intentions of finding fault with the NCTE program. Rather, my purpose is to point out that in both cases the responsibility is placed upon the listeners. NCTE has publicized a list of speakers presenting papers concerning various aspects of their field; this and the points listed above indicate a kind of external organization and direction in which the registrants are invited to participate. Certainly, if the NCTE listeners do not readily engage in dialogue from the floor or in the workshops, leaders will emerge and carry on in order to provide the impetus for discourse. The principles and efforts incorporated here differ only in rhetoric from those behind the Rochester conference; unfortunately, at Rochester, these principles and efforts remained in the "potential" stage. More meaningful discourse and greater flexibility in lecture and group discussion format and scheduling were possible; had the listeners taken more responsibility to facilitate these alterations and to deal with their inoperability within the definition of the conference, they might have satisfied, rather than frustrated, their needs. Questions and comments with regard to each presentation were called for from the lectern; little discussion ensued, however, and no clear definition, necessary to support meaningful dialogue, materialized in several of the small group discussions.

Preoccupation with format and organizational matters left the listeners no room to move, and it created a barrier to many kinds of learning. Are we guilty of dropping out rather than assuming responsibility from within? This is the criticism we make of our students, upon whom we currently depend for discerning and sorting out problems from within our classroom situations.

If the listeners and our students are the oppressed and, therefore, according to Paulo Freire, the only group of people capable of humanizing and helping the oppressor, is it valid for them to employ oppressor tactics in order to accomplish this?

F.   REPORT ON DISCUSSIONS OF GROUP F

Eleanore E. Larson

The discussants in Group F could well be described as thoughtful members of "The Community of Seekers" to which William Pilder referred in his opening remarks. The pattern of discourse was to react to the papers by identifying questions to be explored and expanded. Throughout the four meetings the group focused on these questions:

1. What is or should be the role of the school in our society? (Our persistence in pursuing this alternative should not be interpreted as an attempt to abdicate responsibility; rather, we wondered if we should emphasize efforts to devote energies to the intensive, hard examination of present practice, dedicating ourselves to doing the difficult job of improving our approaches to what Huebner says is a school, not an education, question—teaching reading.)
   a. Is the school doing or trying to do too much, or should it separate out a domain?
   b. Should the school return to or continue to limit its function to the three R's and stop trying to redefine its role?
   c. Is education as represented by the school purposive?
2. Is deschooling the best alternative for our society?
3. Are alternative schools sufficient?
4. How do we modify our naïveté regarding politics of schools?
5. Are the presenters philosophers or curriculum theorists?

We viewed the most valuable function of the discussion group to be the exploring of ideas presented by the speakers, the clarification and testing of our impressions, understandings, and interpretations, and the generation of questions to be studied. We did not try to achieve consensus; nor did we view ourselves as task oriented in regard to mapping out a plan of action to which we would all subscribe.

There was considerable, unresolved disagreement over Starratt's analysis of Schwab's recent position in relation to his plea to call a moratorium on theorizing and alter our emphasis to practical implementation concerns. While there was support for Starratt's position that the vision of the theorist-researcher is critical, the group did not subscribe fully to his conclusion that the practitioner could not perform any of the functions of the theorist. The discussion concluded with the question: Must one be a theorist *or* a practitioner? Meaningful communication between the two endeavors was also encouraged, and it was felt that some realignment of responsibilities of the practitioner could increase his opportunity to contribute to the field of theory. The group concluded that Starratt's review of the current state of the art was a helpful framework for the subsequent papers.

In responding to Huebner's presentation, the group concurred that Huebner's own choice of language provides a poetic experience for the hearer and that his style of expression and presentation is an unusual example of matching the vehicle for communication to the ideas shared; the process served the message. Questions articulated in response to Huebner's paper revealed the group's effort to pursue the predominant concerns stated in the introductory remarks and to relate Huebner's views to them.

Considerable time and concern were devoted to examining whether the dilemma is really one of language, or is it one of delineating problems with which schools can realistically deal? The discussion focused on efforts to clarify, for ourselves, several ideas from Huebner's paper that many of us had not previously viewed as related to educational-school-curriculum inquiry. In particular we tried to project what it would feel and look like if we implemented the imperative to examine metaphor and imagery as essential for survival. We wondered whether examining or analyzing language was in some sense analogous to examining the self.

In our continuing effort to clarify our understanding of Huebner's language, we accepted the imperative that the young must be involved in the examination of language if they are to exercise their right to participate in a public work. It became clear that the thoughtful examination of language could increase our awareness and understanding of the political nature of schooling, and it deserved serious consideration.

To continue our efforts to relate to Huebner's expressed ideas, we discussed whether:

1. We could ever answer: What is of value? What is valuable to conserve? What of the past can be made present for which child in which community?
2. Will there not always be the problem of selection which must be analyzed according to current values?
3. Can the concepts (such as print) be applied in practical form?
4. Is the "answer" as important as the processes and experiences by which we attempt to examine the dilemma?
5. How do we define the relationships between rights and consequences of exercising rights versus rights and responsibilities? Are they mutually exclusive?
6. What are curricular implications depending on our decision regarding #5?
7. Is discipline-control the final result for the child who is a misfit in relation to social or teacher expectations?
8. Are the consequences of assuming and exercising rights discipline and loss of rights?

The group felt Huebner had made a significant contribution to the conference and the field of curriculum theory by exposing us to a domain where little exploring had been done. In so doing, he had greatly expanded our horizons and provided some direction (even tools) for continued efforts.

In turning our attention to the Pinar work, many of us found we had been invited to share in an attempt to relate cultural revolution to curriculum theory. For many this was indeed an initial and introductory exposure to the idea. It was generally agreed that Pinar's description and analysis of the developing ideas, experiences, and rationale for the counterculture "movement" were needed by, and of help to, the participants in permitting them to relate to the proposed "next steps."

Much of the discussion focused on our efforts to clarify and identify with the language and the content. We seemed to need to "hear" ourselves work with the concepts, to see if we did indeed hear what Pinar was expressing, or whether we had the language needed to discuss our concerns. We tried to delineate what we understood, accepted, and questioned.

Whether it was possible to pursue self-understanding in the institutional setting became a major focus for discussion, and we agreed that the institutional setting rarely, if ever, provides resources for solitude. We wondered if this were because solitude is not very high in our sense of priorities. Does this age of accountability make us increasingly skeptical of nonobservable "performance"? Are we threatened because solitude is not viewed as being productive?

Since the way to achieve identity is reflective and contemplative and one cannot find it by looking for it directly, can it be provided through institutional means?

In the search for the unknown, how does one come to grips with one's desire to accept or to reject the movement? To consider this alternative, one must seriously and realistically address the question: How much risk am I going to take in honestly expressing my inner emotions?

Does one find himself by getting lost? Is finding identity transcendentally too individualistic? Is this a process one must experience in order to take "next steps"? Must one remove himself from the group (society) in order to return to the group?

If the change must first occur in the individual, rather than in institutions, can one then come to terms with the institutional context in which he exists? Or, will the changed individual(s) create alternative institutions?

The group urged that we no longer continue to deny or avoid the question: Are schools systemic in inhibiting unique and novel expressions characteristic of youth in their (the schools') narrow attention to producing "products" for society?

In considering Macdonald's presentation, the discussion revealed some confusion and disagreement in regard to his message or whether he really did develop a transcendental developmental ideology. The need for time and possibly help in examining the models and paradigms presented was expressed, and the following questions were raised, but not expanded: Are we ready to develop a theory to look at totality? Does implementation of a theory generally result in fragmentation? As in our earlier sessions but to even a greater degree, we reiterated the presenters' ideas.

One member of the group challenged Macdonald's definition of ideology, claiming that it was useless and going on to state that ideology is a system of life based on the expression of basic beliefs or philosophy out of which grow "pillars"; the partitions between social systems (education, politics, and so forth) are changed in response to a change in philosophical position. He claimed an ideology is developed by a consensus and not formed by the values found in the individual's inner self, which was Macdonald's position.

Also, to a larger extent than in any other session, the group attempted to look at the different points of view of the presenters in relation to each other, to search for both commonality and uniqueness. There was the suggestion that Macdonald supported and utilized the positions of Greene and Pinar, but moved a step beyond them in implementation.

In our discussion of the several presentations these questions were posed but not really pursued: Are the presenters most accurately characterized as philosophers or theorists? Has the movement from outer to inner resources weakened the development of curriculum theory rather than strengthening it? Is retreat a necessary prerequisite to advance?

It does not seem productive to try to summarize the preceding remarks; I would prefer to share some reflections regarding the experience of participating in the conference. During and soon after the conference, I felt primarily overwhelmed by the quality of both presenters' styles and the content of the papers, and yet I was also aware that I had experienced something deep, personal, and private. There was a great need for time to study and think, to try to identify and relate to the development of curriculum theory the wealth of ideas introduced in such a short span of time.

One needed solitude, time to read, to study, and to continue discourse with this "Community of Seekers." The presenters had been courageous and generous in sharing their ideas and proposals and in soliciting reactions, and each participant realized and welcomed the serious responsibility to continue his own inquiry, to increase his understanding, to achieve a degree of perspective from which to compare and contrast the various points of view, to clarify and order his questions, to participate in the continued development of the study of curriculum theory.

I realized that I had been privileged to participate in the conference, and that I had much sorting and searching to do. The challenge now rests with the participant.

G. REFLECTIONS ON THE CONFERENCE

Paul R. Klohr

Tough, nagging questions persist in the minds of many who try to understand the nature and meaning of such complex intellectual constructs as "higher consciousness" or "cultural revolution." And these questions grow in geometric proportion when one attempts to probe possible implications for education and, in particular, for curriculum theory. Those trying to respond and to understand are required to generate for themselves what Thomas Kuhn calls a new paradigm for viewing the world. In effect, it is required, as Don Juan asks of Castaneda, not only that we look but also that we *see*.

Those of us at the Rochester Conference sensed the difficulty of pursuing the meaning and implications of all that we heard in such a short time. There is no simple, clear way to report how we coped with the difficulty. Reflection on the efforts of one group of twelve to fifteen participants may, however, give something of the flavor of our reactions. These efforts are perhaps best caught up in the questions the group tended to pursue, sometimes explicitly but, more often, implicitly, as individuals asked themselves, "What do I make of it?" and, in turn, shared their feelings and views with others.

The questions, once taken out of the context of the group setting in which they were generated, lose some of the richness and uniqueness they exhibited during the conference. In fact, they take on an academic, overly descriptive character that seems to validate one of the central themes running through the papers—namely, we must free our thinking from the conventional conceptual tools now available to us in what Hampden-Turner calls "the borrowed toolbox." We were well aware of this need, but we also recognized the huge, long-term effort that must go into the development of more adequate language forms and modes of seeing, inquiring, reporting. Caught up in the constraints of time and the conventional modes of thinking, we posed for ourselves these kinds of questions:

166

1. What is the nature of the philosophical and psychological under-pinnings of heightened consciousness and cultural revolution?
2. What is (should be) the relationship between social-political ac-tion and heightened consciousness?
3. What community settings (if any) support and nourish the search for heightened consciousness?
4. Can (or should) curriculum theory be reconceived in a new paradigm generated from insight into the nature of conscious-ness and cultural revolution?

These four questions will serve as a rough structure for reporting some of the substantive matters our group identified and discussed. No effort is made to focus on individual papers and the discussion which followed each presentation. Rather, the attempt is to report a kind of synthesis that cuts across all of the papers and involves, in addition, the thinking that group members, themselves, brought to the synthesis. Readers will recognize that this response is almost entirely in the realm that James Macdonald, in an overview done for the *Journal of Educational Research* in 1971, termed a reconceptual-ization of the field. We did not address ourselves to these questions in terms of scientific endeavor or in terms of guidelines for curricu-lum development, two other realms within the field as Macdonald saw it.

PHILOSOPHICAL AND PSYCHOLOGICAL UNDERPINNINGS

From Starratt's opening remarks which, among other things, called for the examination of curriculum in a human, holistic setting to Pilder's closing lines from T. S. Eliot, we were continuously im-pressed with the emergence of a different philosophical-psychological base. To speak of "humanistic" education has become a current cliché. Yet, for want of a more adequate term, we tended to use this adjective to reflect on the basis of the several papers. As we did this, however, we were made aware of a certain risk by Maxine Greene's warning that "to have the plague" might involve being abstract, a common disease of curriculum theorists. She points out that "to use big words like 'humanization,' 'democratization,' 'self-actualiza-tion'" might obscure what is really taking place between the person and his world.

Paul Goodman often issued a similar warning—namely, that professionals must see individuals as persons and not as some highly refined "personnel" category. To keep from falling into this trap, we kept asking: What is happening to *me*? How do *I* feel about this? In effect, we were engaging in the kind of "centering" that Macdonald proposed. This centering seemed inevitably to require each of us to make the inward journey that Huebner, Pinar, and Pilder described as a necessary condition for heightened consciousness. We recognized the necessity of honoring what might ordinarily have been seen as autobiographical data. But we were engaging in this indwelling to emerge and to use ourselves more fully as a basic resource for confronting the world and its problems and, more particularly, issues of curriculum theory in their larger context.

To the extent that this happened for individuals in the group, there was a desirable blend of process and content. We were, indeed, exploring, however primitively, some basic first steps in the generation of more adequate curriculum theory. Those who had such an experience were impressed, time and again, with the great amount of work required to move from new and different foundations for curriculum thinking to the conceptual structures required to make a difference in practical school and community settings.

In a somewhat more cognitive sense, we also became increasingly aware of the philosophical and psychological sources our speakers were using. Polanyi, Merleau-Ponty, Camus, Sartre, James, Jung, Kierkegaard, Marcuse, Roszak—the list goes on and on. In many instances, philosophy and psychology were merged in ways that more conventional philosophers and psychologists refuse to recognize, and there are clear existential overtones throughout these sources. For example, one need only to recall Pilder's use of Kierkegaard's formulation of the nature of consciousness and its relation to despair, Greene's use of metaphors from Camus, or Pinar's use of Sartre's work to sense again the many threads of existentialism woven into the fabric of the papers. And the whole matter of whether Merleau-Ponty or William James or Carl Jung is speaking as a philosopher or as a psychologist becomes simply an academic question. They, like those who spoke at the Rochester Conference, are addressing themselves to fundamental questions of the human condition, questions not bounded by a single discipline.

The language used to investigate problems of education and curriculum often sounds strange. It is strange in the sense that our ears and minds have become accustomed to the conventional in a field dominated by technological terminology. We have not developed ways of thinking about curriculum that Huebner and Macdonald have, for the past ten years or so, urged that we explore—namely, by using the logic of the aesthetic, the social, and the moral disciplines. Nor, as Cremin has pointed out, have we had much direct help from professional philosophers.

For most of us, this conference was, then, an active demonstration of how fresh perspectives can emerge from philosophical and psychological underpinnings that have not yet been fully explored with respect to their implications for curriculum theory. We have witnessed the beginnings of a reconceptualization of curriculum "foundations," if not, indeed, the field itself.

RELATIONSHIP TO SOCIAL-POLITICAL ACTION

Here we were at a "theory" conference trying to focus on possible relationships to action in the larger social arena—not exactly a setting for action! The paradox bothered us all. Pilder confessed that he could not hold the terms *heightened consciousness, cultural revolution,* and *curriculum* together. He, like many of us trying to keep the three in focus, became trapped in the conventional rhetoric used to talk about the relationship between education and social reform. And he would have none of it. Above everything else, this violated, for him, the basic tenet that consciousness is "what is lived," that is, in Polanyi's terms, "more than can be told."

Bateman took the position that education can never be politically neutral, underscoring John Holt's view that good education cannot survive in a bad society. Hence, by its very nature, curriculum making is a social-political act.

Pinar saw the possibilities of a transformation if the efforts that could be called political or social were "conducted self-rememberedly, from one's center as an expression of oneself." This view was echoed in Macdonald's conception of a transcendental ideology that involved a basic "centering" of the person in the world.

In fact, no one of the presentations failed to touch on the many social-political implications of a thorough reconceptualization of curriculum theory and, in turn, of curriculum development. The generalizations one can make in retrospect about this aspect of the papers and the discussion which it generated in the group reflect the dilemma many thoughtful educators now face. Individuals with radical ideas are finding it difficult to get their bearings. How we struggled with this!

The political climate does not favor radical-related ideas and activities as it did, for example, in the 1960's. Conservative forces seem to grow stronger while those proposing radical change seem isolated and relatively powerless. The question of strategy is one of how to make good use of the openings made in the 1960's toward achieving basic societal reconstruction, if, in Holt's terms, we must have a good society in order to have good education.

Frank Riessman has spoken of the problem as one of converting the present period of ebb and reaction into a new period of flow. He, like Alvin Gouldner, proposes that we work hard to generate more adequate theories and use them to transcend the pressures of our particular existence. This transcendence gives others as well as ourselves a vision of social alternatives and the courage to undertake change. In effect, the need is for more adequate theory if we are to engage in the social-political action that is clearly inevitable if we are to take seriously the ideas of heightened consciousness and cultural revolution. The Marxian-based liberal-radical ideology of the post-World War II days is grossly inadequate.

If one can, indeed, generalize about the views of the conference participants this way, one outcome seems clear: extensive additional work needs to be undertaken in what Macdonald called the curriculum development realm in 1971. This is to say that the exploratory theory-building efforts of the Rochester Conference must be transformed into many middle-range curriculum development efforts. These efforts must go beyond an extension of the Deweyan problem-solving approach of the Great Society. This base simply has not been adequate.

One is not required to choose between theory building at the metatheoretical level (the level that characterizes the papers presented at the conference) and theory building that might be characterized as middle range in the development realm. Both levels are crucial if the field of curriculum is to be reconceptualized and if the inevitable relationship to social-political action is to be more fully realized.

SUPPORTIVE COMMUNITY SETTINGS

Much of the writing and discussion one finds when he explores heightened consciousness and cultural revolution gives the picture that community as such has little to do with the inward journey one must make. There tends to be an aura of isolation and loneliness in most descriptions of the personal pilgrimages that are clearly a part of the move to raise one's level of consciousness. Maxine Greene speaks of the "sense of powerlessness expressed in cynicism and privatism, a loss of trust tinged with despair." And most of the literature of education deals with community centers on what Charles Reich would call a Consciousness II mentality. Fred Newmann and Donald Oliver would categorize it as a "Great Society" mentality as contrasted to their "missing society" conception of the nature of community which has trust as a central criterion of the quality of shared life. Small wonder, then, that those disciplines themselves, in attempting to become more fully conscious of who they are and what that means, have difficulty in relating to the idea of community as it has been used in the professional literature of education and cognate fields.

A significant outcome of the Rochester Conference is the fresh realization that the personal pilgrimages involved in seeking heightened consciousness and in participating in the cultural revolution are directly related to community. Or, more precisely, they require a redefinition of community.

Greene makes the point effectively when she states "consciousness does not mean mere innerness or introspection." She continues with the idea that consciousness means a "thrusting towards the things of the world . . . the multiple ways in which the individual comes in touch with objects, events, and other human beings."

Pilder, after describing some aspects of indwelling, states that "to express culture in work demands a shared way of living, a mutual indwelling." He then goes on to point out, along with others, that most institutions, and schools among them, no longer are places where persons can work together because they share a common ground. His notion of mutual indwelling becomes a basic element in the reconceptualization of community—a realm of shared experience that could both support and nourish heightened consciousness and a wide range of cultural differences and life styles.

Huebner emphasizes the need for hermeneutical art which is "the bridge between self and others, a linkage among past, present and future, and the vehicle by which individuals in community arrive at mutual understanding." He sees the individual as being pushed out into "an ongoing community with traditions of care for people and traditions of care for collective or public wealth." Much of what he says in this respect is caught up in his concept of "care for the new being."

In the papers themselves, or in the discussions that followed, there was clearly no resolution of how to develop a redefinition of community, which many agreed was basic. There was no doubt, however, that this was a necessity whether one adopted Pilder's idea of the need for mutual indwelling or Huebner's notion of the hermeneutical.

With some of the participants, the direction suggested by Huebner in his discussion of open education pointed the direction for continued work. He said "open education points to the search for communities, groups of people on pilgrimage ... *reshaping their lives together* and telling and retelling the stories of where they have been and where they seem to be going." How better can one visualize a community setting to nourish and support heightened consciousness and cultural revolution? And in what other setting can more effective curricula be developed?

Again, as with the other pervasive questions that ran through the after-paper discussions, the conference participants were struck with the immensity of the task they faced as they struggled to generate more adequate curriculum theory.

A NEW CURRICULUM THEORY PARADIGM

The fourth question we used to try to bring order to our group reactions differs from the first three not only in substance but also in its syntactical relationship to the others. Having explored the first three questions in terms of the rich content of the papers and our somewhat primitive extension of that content because of the constraints of time, we are convinced that there are indeed fresh, unique perspectives to be gained from a cultivation of insight into the nature of consciousness and cultural revolution. We view these insights as foundations for the generation of new paradigms for curriculum theory.

We use paradigms in this context the way Thomas Kuhn uses the concept in his brilliant effort to explain the nature of scientific revolutions. It is similar to the sense in which Willis W. Harmon speaks of the need for new conceptual structures appropriate for a metanoia, or major cultural shift. Lewis Mumford also catches up some of the spirit of our discourse when he projects some dimensions of his regime of plentitude as does Roszak in his sketching of some aspects of rhapsodic intellect. George Leonard simply speaks of a transformation.

Whatever we call it, we sensed the pressing need to develop different modes of experiencing life and translating such experience into personal-political-social language forms that might be shared with others. The unfinished work-in-progress quality of the presentations gives each of us some sense of what is involved in being a generator of curriculum theory as contrasted, for example, with a consumer of the theory of others. We can see something of the personal struggle involved, the despair, the paradoxes, the excitement, the unfinished questions yet to be faced. Sensing this struggle gives us courage to try to make the pilgrimage ourselves. Not all of us will finally want to do this, but some will. What more can one ask but that those who do want to join hands and move ahead? The road is far from clear, but the Rochester Conference points out some directions.